SEPT. 2014

"In his fresh, engaging manner, Mark Batterson invites us to revisit the messages and miracles of Christ. I am privileged to know Mark and the wonderful people he serves at National Community Church in Washington, DC. I am thankful for him, for them, and now for this wonderful book. Our Christian convictions are only as valid as Christ Himself. Mark reminds us that faith in Jesus is worth the risk."

—**Max Lucado**, pastor and bestselling author

"Mark Batterson shows us how to open our eyes to the miraculous and, in doing so, truly see that the One who walked on water and raised people from the dead is still working miracles today."

—**Pastor Rick Warren**, founding pastor of Saddleback Church and founder of the P.E.A.C.E. Plan initiative

"If Mark Batterson can't convince you that our God still performs miracles, I doubt anyone could. This book is bound to stoke the fire of your faith, even if all you have left are a few weak embers."

—**Roma Downey and Mark Burnett**, executive producers of *The Bible* miniseries and *Son of God*

THE
GRAVE
ROBBER

THE GRAVE ROBBER

HOW JESUS CAN MAKE
YOUR IMPOSSIBLE POSSIBLE

MARK BATTERSON

BakerBooks

a division of Baker Publishing Group
Grand Rapids, Michigan

© 2014 by Mark Batterson

Published by Baker Books
a division of Baker Publishing Group
P.O. Box 6287, Grand Rapids, MI 49516-6287
www.bakerbooks.com

Printed in the United States of America

Library of Congress Cataloging-in-Publication Data is on file at the Library of Congress, Washington, DC.

ISBN 978-0-8010-1594-6 (cloth)
ISBN 978-0-8010-1599-1 (ITPE)

The author is represented by Fedd & Company, Inc.

14 15 16 17 18 19 20   7 6 5 4 3 2 1

Dedicated to the Grave Robber
and to those who will discover Him for the
first time in the pages of this book

Contents

Don't Miss the Miracle
  1. The Day Water Blushed   13
  2. Miraculous   15
  3. The Lost Miracles   22

The First Sign
  4. The Wine Maker   33
  5. Six Stone Jars   43
  6. One Nudge   54

The Second Sign
  7. Supernatural Synchronicity   65
  8. God Speed   81
  9. The Seventh Hour   90

The Third Sign
  10. Very Superstitious   101
  11. Self-Fulfilling Prophecies   112
  12. The Rule Breaker   122

Contents

The Fourth Sign
13. Two Fish   135
14. Lord Algebra   145
15. Count the Fish   156

The Fifth Sign
16. The Water Walker   169
17. Dare the Devil   179
18. Cut the Cable   189

The Sixth Sign
19. Never Say Never   201
20. The Miracle League   211
21. Spit on It   223

The Seventh Sign
22. The Grave Robber   233
23. Even Now   240
24. Risk Your Reputation   252
25. One Little Yes   262

Acknowledgments   265
Notes   267

Don't Miss the Miracle

No one could perform the signs you are doing if God were not with him.

John 3:2

1

THE DAY WATER BLUSHED

FOR NEARLY THIRTY years, the One who had crafted the universe with His voice crafted furniture with His hands. And He was good at what He did—no crooked table legs ever came out of the carpenter's shop in Nazareth.[1] But Jesus was more than a master carpenter. He was also God incognito. His miraculous powers rank as history's best-kept secret for nearly three decades, but all that changed the day water blushed in the face of its Creator.

That was the day the woodbender became a waterbender. Jesus manipulated the molecular structure of water and turned it into wine—757 bottles, no less. And nothing but the best. This wasn't just wine, it was fine wine.

Sometimes God shows up. Sometimes God shows off.

That's what Jesus did on the third day of a wedding feast in Cana, and that was just the beginning. Thirty-four distinct miracles are recorded in the Gospels, while countless more went unrecorded. John's Gospel spotlights seven miracles, unveiling seven dimensions of Jesus' miraculous power. Like the sun rising in the east, each miracle reveals another ray of God's glory until Lazarus steps out of the shadow of his tomb and into the light of the Grave Robber.

The seven miracles are seven signs, and each sign points straight to Jesus. You may be reading this book because you need a miracle. Don't we all at some point in our lives? And God wants to do *now* what He did *then*. But this is more than a course in miracles. It's a book about the only One who can perform them. So let me offer a word of caution at the outset:

Don't seek miracles.

Follow Jesus.

And if you follow Jesus long enough and far enough, you'll eventually find yourself in the middle of some miracles.

Everyone wants a miracle. But here's the catch: no one wants to be in a situation that necessitates one! Of course, you can't have one without the other.

The prerequisite for a miracle is a problem, and the bigger the problem, the greater the potential miracle. If the wedding party in Cana hadn't run out of wine, there would have been no need for the Wine Maker to do what He did. What the bride and groom perceived as a problem was really a perfect opportunity for God to reveal His glory. And nothing has changed since Jesus turned water into wine, healed a man born blind, or called Lazarus out of his tomb four days after his funeral.

He is the God who can make your impossible possible!

2

MIRACULOUS

O N A JANUARY morning in 2007, a world-class violinist played six of Johann Sebastian Bach's most stirring concertos for the solo violin on a three-hundred-year-old Stradivarius worth $3.5 million. Two nights before, Joshua Bell had performed a sold-out concert where patrons gladly paid $200 for nosebleed seats, but this time the performance was free.

Bell ditched his tux with coattails, donned a Washington Nationals baseball cap, and played incognito outside the L'Enfant Plaza Metro station. Street musicians are not an uncommon sight or sound for Washingtonians. In fact, my son Parker has played his guitar outside Metro stations a time or two, trying to make a little extra spending cash. Amazingly, his tip jar fared about as well as that of virtuoso Joshua Bell.

The experiment was originally conceived by *Washington Post* columnist Gene Weingarten and filmed by hidden camera. Of the 1,097 people who passed by, only seven stopped to listen. The forty-five-minute performance ended without applause or acknowledgment. Joshua Bell netted $32.17 in tips, which included a $20 spot from the one person who recognized the Grammy Award–winning musician.[1]

On an average workday nearly a million passengers ride Washington's Metro system, and L'Enfant Plaza is one of the busiest stops. A stampede of tourists and government employees hustle and bustle through turnstiles, trying to get where they're going as quickly as possible. But those circumstances don't discredit or disqualify the question raised by this social experiment: If we do not have a moment to stop and listen to one of the greatest musicians in the world, playing some of the finest music ever written, on one of the most beautiful instruments ever made, how many similarly sublime moments do we miss out on during a normal day?

Remember the old adage? *Beauty is in the eye of the beholder.* It's true of everything, isn't it? But it's especially true of miracles. Miracles are happening all around us all the time, but you won't see them if you don't know how to look for them.

The Invisible Gorilla

Christopher Chabris and Daniel Simons conducted an experiment at Harvard University more than a decade ago that became infamous in psychology circles. Their book *The Invisible Gorilla* popularized it. And you may be one of the millions of viewers who made their Selective Attention Test one of YouTube's most-watched videos.[2]

The two researchers filmed students passing basketballs while moving in a circular fashion. In the middle of the short film, a woman dressed in a gorilla suit walks into the frame, beats her chest, and walks out of the frame. The sequence takes nine seconds in the minute-long video. Viewers are given specific instructions: "Count the number of passes by players wearing white shirts." Of course, the researchers were not interested in their pass-counting ability. They wanted to see if the viewers would notice something they weren't looking for, something as obvious as a gorilla. Amazingly, half of the test group did not.

How is that even possible?

How do you miss the gorilla in the room?

The short answer is *inattentional blindness.*

Inattentional blindness is the failure to notice something in your field of vision because you are focused on something else, in this case people in white shirts passing basketballs. But the first-century Pharisees make an even better case study. They were so focused on Sabbath law that they couldn't see the miracles happening right in front of their eyes. Jesus healed an invalid who hadn't walked in thirty-eight years, gave sight to a man born blind, and restored a man's withered arm. But the Pharisees missed the miracle, and missed the Messiah, because they were blinded by their legalism. They couldn't see past their religious assumptions.

Inattentional blindness can be as intentional as *turning a blind eye to something you don't want to see*, like the Pharisees did. It can also be as unintentional as *fading awareness of the constants in your life that you take for granted over time*. Either way, it's one of the greatest threats to spiritual vitality. One of the truest tests of spiritual maturity is seeing the miraculous in the monotonous.

Monotonous Miracles

Thomas Carlyle, the nineteenth-century Scottish essayist, likened it to a man living his entire life in a cave and then stepping outside to witness the sunrise for the very first time.

Carlyle hypothesized that the caveman would watch with rapt astonishment the sight we daily witness with indifference. In the words of G. K. Chesterton:

> Grown-up people are not strong enough to exult in monotony. Is it possible God says every morning, "Do it again" to the sun; and every evening, "Do it again" to the moon? The repetition in nature may not be a mere recurrence; it may be a theatrical encore.[3]

A few years ago an exchange student from India attended National Community Church. When meteorologists issued a winter storm warning for the DC area, he set his alarm clock for three o'clock in the morning so he wouldn't miss his first snowfall. Then he went outside, all by himself, and made snow angels in the freshly fallen snow. He almost got frostbite because he didn't wear a jacket, a hat, or gloves. He told me he had no idea snow was that cold and that wet. At first I simply chuckled at the thought. But the more I thought about it, the more convicted I felt. I completely ignored something he thoroughly celebrated.

When was the last time you made snow angels in the freshly fallen snow? Or watched the sunrise as an act of worship? Or marveled over a sleeping child? Or stared into the starry night sky? Or relished the laugh of a loved one?

There is nothing like experiencing something for the first time, whether it's your first snow or first kiss. The first time is unforgettable. There is a miraculous quality to new experiences that makes time stand still—a sneak peek of what eternity will be like.

God has wired us in such a way that we're hypersensitive to new stimuli, but over time the cataracts of the customary cloud our vision. We lose our awareness of the miraculous, and with it, the awe of God.

A Celestial 360

You may feel as if you are sitting still right now, but it's an illusion of miraculous proportions. Planet Earth is spinning around its axis at a speed of 1,000 miles per hour. Every 24 hours, planet Earth pulls off a celestial 360. We're also hurtling through space at an average velocity of 67,108 miles per hour. That's not just faster than a speeding bullet. It's 87 times faster than the speed of sound. So even on a day when you feel like you didn't get much done, don't forget that you did travel 1,599,793 miles through space! To top things off, the Milky Way is spinning like a galactic pinwheel at the dizzying rate of 483,000 mph.[4]

If that isn't miraculous, I don't know what is.

Yet when was the last time you thanked God for keeping us in orbit? I'm guessing never! "Lord, I wasn't sure we'd make the full rotation today, but You did it again!" We just don't pray that way. And that is the ultimate irony: we already believe God for the big miracles like they're no big deal. The trick is trusting Him for the little ones like healing an incurable illness, finding Ms. Right, opening a deadbolt door of opportunity, or getting us out of what seems like insurmountable debt.

Compared to keeping the planets in orbit, how big is your biggest dream? How bad is your worst problem? How difficult is your greatest challenge?

Microscopic Miracles

You don't have to look through a telescope to spy the miraculous. You can put it under a microscope too. Trillions of chemical reactions are taking place in your body every second of every day—you are inhaling oxygen, metabolizing energy, managing equilibrium, manufacturing hormones, fighting antigens, filtering stimuli, mending tissue, purifying toxins, digesting food, and circulating blood. All the while your brain is performing up to ten quadrillion calculations per second using only ten watts of power.[5] A computer would require a gigawatt of power produced by a nuclear power plant to pull off the same performance.

Yet I know people, and you do too, who say they have never experienced a miracle. Nothing could be further from the truth. You have never not! You aren't just surrounded by miracles. You are one.

Keep looking under that microscope; things are about to get even more interesting.

If your personal genome sequence was written out long-hand, it would be a three-billion-word book. The King James Version of the Bible has 783,137 words, so your genetic code is the equivalent of nearly four thousand Bibles. And if your personal genome sequence were an audio book and you were read at a rate of one double helix per second, it would take nearly a century to put you into words!

Psalm 139:13–14 reads:

> You knit me together in my mother's womb.
> I praise you because I am fearfully and wonderfully
>   made.

Those are some of the most poetic and prophetic words in the Bible. They may be some of the oldest too. While most scholars attribute Psalm 139 to David, one rabbinic tradition says it goes all the way back to Adam.[6] If that is true, these are some of the oldest and truest words in the history of humankind.

Every moment of every day, we experience the miraculous on both a microscopic and macroscopic scale. Miracles are happening all around us all the time. But the greatest miracle is the one you see in the mirror. There never has been and never will be anyone like you. Of course, that isn't a testament to you. It's a testament to the God who created you.

3

THE LOST MIRACLES

THE LARGEST LIBRARY in the world is three blocks from my office.

Founded in 1800, the Library of Congress was originally housed in the Capitol building until the British burned it to the ground during the War of 1812.[1] Its three thousand volumes helped kindle the fire. On January 30, 1815, Congress set out to rebuild the nation's library by approving the purchase of the largest personal collection of books in the United States, belonging to our third president, Thomas Jefferson. Jefferson once quipped, "I cannot live without books."[2] But apparently he was willing to part with his 6,487 volumes for a lump sum of $23,950.

Along with its current collection of 35 million books, the Library of Congress is the custodian of 13.6 million photographs, 6.5 million pieces of sheet music, and 5.4 million maps. Its 838 miles of bookshelves, if placed end to end, would stretch all the way from Washington, DC, to Granite City, Illinois. Every day it's open, the library adds 11,000 new items to its collections. Housed within its vaults is one of only three perfect copies of the Gutenberg Bible; *The Bay Psalm Book*, the first extant book printed in the United States in 1640; "America's Birth Certificate," the 1507 world map by Martin Waldseemüller on which the name *America* appears for the first time; and the world's largest collection of historical phone books where you can find the street address and five-digit phone number of your great-great-grandparents.

One of the lesser-known books in Jefferson's collection, but maybe the most significant of all, was printed in Geneva, Switzerland, in 1555. It radically changed the way we read the Bible. The French printer and scholar Robert Estienne had the novel idea of adding numbers to create chapters and verses. So the next time you cite Psalm 23 or Romans 8:28 or Ephesians 3:20, you have Robert Estienne's *Biblia* to thank for it. He also made "John 3:16" signs at sporting events possible!

While it's nothing more than historical conjecture, I can't help but wonder if Estienne's unique translation of Scripture is what inspired Thomas Jefferson to invent his own version— *The Jefferson Bible*. But instead of adding numbers, Jefferson cut verses out. He created an abridged Bible by removing the miracles.

The Chopping Block

Thomas Jefferson had a profound appreciation for the teachings of Jesus, but Jefferson was also a child of the Enlightenment. When Jefferson was a sixteen-year-old first-year student at the College of William and Mary, Professor William Small introduced him to the writings of the British empiricists. John Locke, Sir Francis Bacon, and their enlightened brethren enthroned reason and made logic lord. Jefferson did likewise.

In February 1804, Jefferson went to work with a razor. He clipped his favorite passages out of his Bible and pasted them in double columns on forty-six octavo sheets. Jefferson included the teachings of Jesus but excluded the miracles. He deleted the virgin birth, the resurrection, and every supernatural event in between. In the words of historian Edwin Gaustad, "If a moral lesson was embedded in a miracle, the lesson survived in Jeffersonian scripture, but the miracle did not. Even when this took careful cutting with scissors."[3] The story of the man with the withered hand is a classic example. In Jefferson's Bible, Jesus still offers commentary on the Sabbath, but the man's hand is left unhealed. When Jefferson got to John's Gospel, Gaustad notes, he "kept his blade busy."[4] Jefferson's version of the Gospels ends with the stone rolled in front of the tomb. Jesus died on the cross but never rose from the dead.

Hard to imagine, isn't it—taking scissors to the sacred text of Scripture? But don't we do the very same thing? We wouldn't dare use a razor, but we cut and paste nonetheless. We pick and choose our favorite verses while ignoring the texts we cannot comprehend or don't particularly like. We rationalize the verses that are too radical. We scrub down the verses that are too supernatural. We put Scripture on the chopping block of human logic and end up with a neutered gospel. We commit intellectual idolatry, creating God in our image. So instead of living a life that resembles the supernatural standard set in Scripture, we follow an abridged version of the Bible that looks an awful lot like us.

The Boldest Statement in the Bible

When you subtract the miracles like Thomas Jefferson did, you're left with a very wise yet weak Jesus. I'm afraid this is the

Jesus many people follow. He's kind and compassionate, but the raw power is missing in action. So we follow His teachings but never experience His miracles. And that doesn't just fall short of the standard He set—it misses the point altogether.

One of the boldest statements in the Bible is found in John 14:12:

> Whoever believes in me will do the works I have been doing, and they will do even greater things than these.

Greater things? It would sound like heresy if it didn't come from the lips of Jesus. It's one of those verses that we tend to rationalize, so let me tell you exactly what it means. If you follow Jesus, you'll do what He did. You'll seek to please the heavenly Father first and foremost. You'll care for the poor, you'll wash feet, and you'll offend some Pharisees along the way. You'll also traffic in the miraculous. And it won't just be as an eyewitness. It'll be as a catalyst. Please believe me when I say, *you are someone else's miracle!*

Make no mistake about it: *only God can perform miracles.* So God gets all of the glory. But as you'll see in the pages to follow, nearly every miracle has a human element. Sometimes you need to step into the Jordan River, like the priests of Israel, before God will part the waters.[5] And sometimes you need to wade into the Jordan seven times, like Naaman.[6] Only God could miraculously heal Naaman's leprosy, but he would have forfeited the miracle if he hadn't positioned himself for it by repeated obedience. So while some miracles take only a single step of faith, others require multiple attempts! But whether it's ankle deep or waist deep, you've got to wade into the Jordan River. Sometimes you've got to do the natural before God will do the supernatural.

The playground we live on, planet Earth, was designed with natural boundaries that mark the outer limits of human possibility. The speed of light is the fence line, and the laws of nature are the fence posts. Some of them are well-known, like the law of gravity or Newton's three laws of motion. Others are more obscure, like Bell's theorem. While those fence posts are constantly being repositioned by scientific research, they establish a borderline between what is possible and what is impossible. It's the invisible, impassable fence between the natural and the supernatural, and no human can dig under it, climb over it, or walk around it. But God has put a gate in the fence. His name is Jesus.

If you follow Jesus long enough and far enough, you'll eventually trespass into the impossible. You'll turn water into wine, feed five thousand with two fish, and walk on water. I'm not suggesting that you go walk off the nearest dock and see how many steps you can take. God will probably manifest His power very differently for you than He did for the original disciples. But if you believe what Jesus said, then you'll do what Jesus did. The miracles you experience should be even greater than the miracles Jesus performed, in terms of both quantity and quality. And the miracles you'll encounter in the pages that follow substantiate that statement.

Trip Wires

Before unveiling the seven signs, let me identify two trip wires that keep us from stepping into the miraculous. The first is subliminal skepticism.

Miracles, by definition, are a violation of natural laws. And like well-trained trial lawyers, we instinctively object to any such violation. Why? Because miracles aren't logical. And our natural tendency is to explain away what we cannot explain.

If you've ever flipped through the religious channels on television, you've probably seen a charlatan or two. Some false teachers make promises the Bible doesn't back up. Or maybe you've even witnessed someone try to manufacture a miracle. If you've ever been hoodwinked, skepticism can linger like a low-grade fever. But counterfeit miracles don't negate the genuine article. In fact, counterfeits hint at the real McCoy. Remember, Satan disguises himself as an angel of light. So let me ask you: Does the existence of false angels, known as fallen angels, negate the existence of real angels? I would argue the opposite. And I would say the same of false miracles.

There is a fine line between discernment and skepticism. Discernment is filtering what is false from what is true with the help of Holy Scripture and the Holy Spirit. Skepticism is a predisposition toward disbelief that is prejudiced by past experience. Skeptics throw the baby out with the bathwater because they cannot filter out what is false. The Bible is our filter. If something doesn't pass the filter test, spit it out. But don't let the existence of what is false keep you from believing what is true. And the truth is this: God can do now what He did then. If you cut the miracles out, you cut Christianity off at the knees.

The second trip wire is dormant disappointment.

Maybe you've prayed for a miracle, but it feels like God didn't hear a word you had to say. I can't explain why some prayers aren't answered when we ask or why some miracles don't happen the way we want. But it's a mistake to allow a single disappointment to make you throw in the miracle towel altogether. Disappointment is a knee-jerk reaction—we pull back on the reins of faith because we don't want to feel the sting of disappointment again.

This is so subtle, yet so significant. So let me paint a picture.

In 1911 a Swiss psychologist named Édouard Claparède was treating a forty-seven-year-old patient with no short-term memory. At the beginning of every appointment, they would customarily shake hands. Then one day Claparède decided to perform a little experiment. When his patient reached out her hand to shake his, he had a pin concealed in his hand, and he stuck her with it. She quickly withdrew her hand in pain. A few minutes later, she had no memory of the pin-prick. But from that moment on, she would not shake hands with Claparède. She wasn't sure why, but she felt like she couldn't completely trust him. The residue of pain kept her from reaching her hand out.[7]

Think of disappointment as a pinprick. It hurts. And when we experience a disappointment of the faith variety, many of us stop reaching our hand toward God. We pull back. We can't identify why we don't completely trust God, but our dormant disappointment keeps us from reaching out in faith.

I don't think you need to lie on a counselor's couch and identify the genesis of every doubt and disappointment. But if you're going to experience the miraculous, you have to confront the dormant disappointments in your past.

Remember the man who said to Jesus, "I believe; help my unbelief"?[8]

That's all of us, isn't it?

We experience an internal tug-of-war between belief and unbelief. My hope is that this book tugs you toward the miraculous. And that's precisely why John writes his Gospel of miracles:

> But these are written that you may believe that Jesus is the Messiah, the Son of God, and that by believing you may have life in his name.[9]

The Seven Signs

The single greatest miracle is the forgiveness of sin made possible through the crucifixion and resurrection of the sinless

Son of God. There is no close second. That miracle is available to anyone, anytime. And it's the only miracle we *must* experience if we want to spend eternity with the heavenly Father. But the miracle of salvation isn't the finish line. It's the baseline.

In John 2, water molecules recognize the voice of the One who called them into existence. Like every atom in the universe, they submit to His ultimate authority. In John 4, Jesus heals a nobleman's son long-distance, revealing His lordship over latitude and longitude. Then, in John 5, He reveals His mastery over chronology, reversing thirty-eight years of pain and suffering with one command. In John 6, Jesus introduces a new miraculous equation: $5 + 2 = 5,000$ R12. His encore is waltzing across the waves on the Sea of Galilee. In John 9, there is more to the miracle than meets the eye. Jesus doesn't just heal a blind man's eyes; He hard-wires a blind man's brain by creating a synaptic pathway between his optic nerve and visual cortex. And just when you think you've seen it all, the Grave Robber turns a tomb into a waiting room. In John 11, Jesus robs the Grim Reaper by calling Lazarus out of the tomb four days after he has died.

As Oliver Wendell Holmes once said, when a person's mind is stretched by a new idea, it never returns to its original dimensions.[10] Our exploration of the seven miracles in John's Gospel will stretch your mind, but I pray it will also stretch your faith. That was John's original intent. The miracles of Jesus are more than *facts* of history. Every miracle is a microcosm. They don't just reveal what Jesus *did*, past tense. They reveal what He wants to *do* in your life, present tense. What He's done before, He wants to do again. And if we do what the disciples did in the Bible, God will do what He did.

Turning water into wine was epic, but it was just the beginning. Each of the seven miracles in John's Gospel is more amazing than the last one. Each one reveals a little more power, a little more glory. Then the Grave Robber shows up and shows off His death-defying power. But that's just the start. The seventh miracle is *not* the epilogue. It's the prologue to the miracles Jesus wants to do in your life. And when you experience a miracle, the way you steward it is by believing God for even bigger and better miracles.

Let the miracles begin.

THE FIRST SIGN

On the third day a wedding took place at Cana in Galilee. Jesus' mother was there, and Jesus and his disciples had also been invited to the wedding. When the wine was gone, Jesus' mother said to him, "They have no more wine."

"Woman, why do you involve me?" Jesus replied. "My hour has not yet come."

His mother said to the servants, "Do whatever he tells you."

Nearby stood six stone water jars, the kind used by the Jews for ceremonial washing, each holding from twenty to thirty gallons.

Jesus said to the servants, "Fill the jars with water"; so they filled them to the brim.

Then he told them, "Now draw some out and take it to the master of the banquet."

They did so, and the master of the banquet tasted the water that had been turned into wine. He did not realize where it had come from, though the servants who had drawn the water knew. Then he called the bridegroom aside and said, "Everyone brings out the choice wine first and then the cheaper wine after the guests have had too much to drink; but you have saved the best till now."

John 2:1–10

4

THE WINE MAKER

On the third day a wedding took place at Cana in Galilee.

John 2:1

THERE ARE DAYS.

Then there are days that define the rest of your life.

Some follow a predictable path, like the middle aisle of a church on your wedding day. Others are as unpredictable as a blind date. Either way you aren't who you were just a moment before. In a split second, life is divided into BC and AD. The bridge to the past is forever destroyed, and the future rushes in like a flash flood.

It's a new day.

It's a new normal.

It's the first day of the rest of your life.

This was that day for Jesus. For nearly thirty years Jesus had worked in His father's carpentry shop. For as long as he could remember, people had called him a carpenter. But on the third day of a weeklong wedding feast, this cabinetmaker became the Wine Maker.

Flashback

Thirty-four distinct miracles are recorded in the Gospels. This curriculum vitae excludes the Big Three—the conception, resurrection, and ascension of Christ. And John himself notes in the very last verse of his Gospel that countless other miracles didn't make the *SportsCenter* Top Ten. But John chooses seven miraculous highlights, four of which are only found in the Gospel bearing his name. Each of those seven signs reveals a new dimension of God's power, of God's personality. And each one is more amazing than the last. But before fast-forwarding, we must rewind eighteen years to a defining moment that happened when Jesus was just twelve years old.

The Gospel of Luke gives us our only glimpse of the boy wonder—one lonely snapshot in the family photo album from birth to thirty. But this one peek into His personality is like a theatrical trailer that foreshadows His future.

Our strongest memories often come from unusual moments that take place within otherwise familiar traditions. When those opposites intersect, it's unforgettable. For Jesus, the unusual moment happened during the family's sixty-three-mile pilgrimage from Nazareth to Jerusalem for the Feast of the Passover.

These annual sojourns resulted in countless childhood memories, but one moment became legend in their family folklore. Even as adults, his siblings would tease Jesus mercilessly about the day He missed the bus back to Nazareth. They would laugh about it the rest of their lives, but it wasn't funny when it happened. Fear flew through the minds of Joseph and Mary when their twelve-year-old went missing for three days! When they finally tracked Him down, Jesus was sitting in the temple courts, schooling the most brilliant minds in ancient Israel.

And all who heard him were amazed at his understanding.[1]

He made such a profound impression that some of those very same religious leaders would undoubtedly recognize Jesus two decades later, despite the beard and voice change. Others would plot against His life, threatened by the spiritual prowess of the childhood prodigy turned miracle maker.

For those who know Him as the Son of God, it can be difficult to think of Jesus in human terms. But to fully appreciate His divinity, you cannot depreciate His humanity. Jesus had to be potty-trained like every baby before Him. He had to learn reading, writing, and arithmetic like the rest of us. Jesus had to learn the names of the constellations He created and the laws of nature He engineered. And just like us, Jesus had to discover His destiny through a relationship with His heavenly Father.

Scripture doesn't tell us how or when or where Jesus recognized that He had the power to do the miraculous, but I'm certain it wasn't at a wedding feast in Cana. I don't want to read anything into Scripture that isn't there, but I wouldn't be surprised if Jesus practiced a few of His miracles before they became His profession. He may have healed a few childhood friends while no one was watching, carved a few pieces of wood with nothing more than His mind, or turned water into any number of substances before He turned it into wine.

From an early age Jesus knew what He was capable of. So did Mary. That's why His miraculous powers rank as one of the best-kept secrets in the history of humankind. It wasn't as easy as putting on a pair of glasses a la Clark Kent or wearing a mask like Bruce Wayne. Yet somehow Jesus managed to masquerade as an ordinary carpenter until the wedding at Cana. And the Oscar goes to Jesus!

How hard would it have been to stay His power for thirty years? To restrain Himself when skeptics scoffed or bullies goaded? To stay on the cross when legions of angels were at His beck and call?

Yet Jesus held His hand. And that may be the greatest miracle of all. His power to perform miracles is awe-inspiring, but the willpower to *not* do what He was capable of doing is even more impressive.

The same is true for us. Sometimes the greatest miracle is restraint: holding your tongue or resisting temptation or keeping your temper in check. And Jesus set the standard before a kangaroo court of false accusers. Instead of cursing His executioners, He said, "Father, forgive them, for they know not what they do."[2]

It was love that led Jesus to the cross. It was willpower that kept Him nailed there.

Story Line

My friend Donald Miller is a prolific author. His *New York Times* bestseller *Blue Like Jazz* has breathed rare publishing air, selling more than a million and a half copies. For the record, my personal favorite in his corpus is *A Million Miles in a Thousand Years*. The offshoot of that book is a company Don founded called Storyline. Its purpose is Donald's passion: to help people tell better stories with their lives.

Don recently spoke at National Community Church and shared a defining moment in his own story line. During his teenage years he was somewhat of a misfit. Actually his self-assessment is far more blunt: "I wasn't good at anything." Then Don was asked to write a short article for his high school youth group newsletter. That's when one offhanded compliment rewrote his story line. Someone simply said, "Don, you're a really good writer." It was the first time anyone had told Don he was good at anything.

"There is always one moment in childhood," observed English playwright Graham Greene, "when the door opens and lets the future in."[3]

For me, the door opened during a sophomore speech class in high school. I gave what amounted to a salvation sermon as my final project. I don't think any of my classmates got converted, but that speech became an inciting incident in my story line. Unbeknownst to me, my mom gave a copy of that speech to my grandma, who gave a copy to her Bible study teacher. The Bible study teacher gave it much higher marks than my speech teacher! Then he asked my grandma, "Has Mark ever thought about ministry?" At that point in my plot, the answer was no. It wasn't in my original script. I hadn't given ministry a second thought until this compliment was relayed from my grandma to my mom to me.

Never underestimate the power of one well-timed compliment. It has the power to change a person's entire perspective on life. It has the potential to change a person's plotline for eternity. The right word at the right time can be the catalyst for someone else's miracle.

The twelve-year-old Jesus heard what was said about Him. And just like His mother, He treasured those words in His heart.[4] On long afternoons in the carpenter's shop, Jesus had flashbacks to the day the door opened and let the future in. I suspect He daydreamed more than a few miracles too.

Clues

If you look back on your own history, you'll discover that destiny leaves clues.

Architects built cities out of Legos. Saleswomen sold enough Thin Mints Girl Scout cookies to feed the country of Liechtenstein. Entrepreneurs cornered the lemonade stand market on their cul-de-sac. Entertainers owned the Eurythmics in Guitar Hero. And teachers set up makeshift blackboards and lectured their stuffed animals.

Joel Buckner is a gifted singer-songwriter and one of our incredibly anointed worship leaders at National Community Church. He shared his story with our family over dinner recently. Like for Jesus, the door opened for Joel when he was twelve. He sang "In Christ Alone" by Michael English at his church and made his mama cry. I'm pretty sure his heavenly Father shed a tear of joy too! Nothing makes God happier than when we use our God-given gifts to glorify Him.

I can only imagine the smile on the heavenly Father's face when Jesus turned water into wine. Like watching your son hit his first home run or your daughter get her first ovation at a recital, the first miracle resulted in pure parental pride. I imagine the Father turning to the nearest angel and saying, "That's My boy!"

When you fixate on your sin instead of His forgiveness, it's easy to forget the fact that you are the apple of His eye. We mistakenly think of ourselves as lower in importance than the lilies of the valley or the birds of the air, but in God's taxonomy we're just a little lower than the angels![5] And it doesn't take a miracle to make our heavenly Father proud. Sometimes all it takes is something as simple as honoring your earthly mother.

Hold that thought.

Saving Face

The door to the future cracked open when Jesus was twelve, but He went off the grid for eighteen years. Then the door reopened when the wet bar closed. I don't know if the wedding planner bought too little or if the guests drank too much, but I'm sure a mini-crisis occurred when the bride and groom found out. Running out of wine might seem like a minor problem in the grand scheme of things, but in first-century Palestine it would have resulted in public shame. Plus, your wedding day is the one day you want everything to be perfect. It probably sparked their first marital spat. Can't you hear the muffled tones at the head table? *All I asked you to do was stock the bar with beverages! That's it. You knew how many people were on the guest list. And I even gave you a wine list. How could you go cheapskate on our wedding day?*

Enter Jesus.

I love the fact that this first miracle of Jesus is not about saving a life. It's about saving face! And it reveals how much God cares about the minute details of our lives. God is great not just because nothing is *too big*. God is great because nothing is *too small*. If it's a big deal to you, it's a big deal to God.

A few years ago I had the privilege of speaking at the Church of the Highlands in Birmingham, Alabama. While I was there, I toured their Dream Center in downtown Birmingham to get some ideas for our Dream Center in Washington, DC. They have an amazing ministry to prostitutes, just like Jesus did. Those prostitutes know where to turn when they have a problem. And I heard an amazing story about one of them.

One morning, as the director of the Dream Center was walking out her front door on the way to work, she felt a prompting to go back and grab a pair of woolly socks. It was so strange that she figured it might just be God. So she tucked a pair of woolly socks in her purse and drove down to the Dream Center. She arrived to find a prostitute passed out on the front step. She carried the woman inside and called 911. As she held this prostitute in her arms, the woman slowly regained consciousness. That's when she asked her, "If I could get you anything, what would it be?" Without hesitation, the shivering woman said, "A pair of woolly socks." Come on, what are the chances? That's when she reached in her purse and pulled out her pair of woolly socks. The woman smiled and said, "They even match my outfit."

Why don't miracles like that happen more often? One simple reason: we aren't dialed in to the still small voice of the Holy Spirit. The Holy Spirit is the tuning fork, but we must learn to listen to and obey those Spirit-inspired promptings. If we do, we'll find ourselves in the middle of miracles all the time!

My friend and mentor Dick Foth has been preaching for nearly fifty years, but something happened to him recently that had never happened before. Right in the middle of a message, Dick sensed in his spirit that someone in the congregation was on the verge of an affair. That impression came out of nowhere, and what Dick did was out of character. He stopped preaching and said, "There is someone here who has set themselves up to have an affair. The pieces are in place, and you were planning on making the decision today. Don't do it." Then Dick picked his sermon back up right where he'd left off. After the service, a middle-aged man gave Dick a big bear hug. As they embraced, he whispered in Dick's ear, "That was me! Thank you."

If Dick had kept on preaching and ignored the prompting, he would have missed the miracle. But when you obey those promptings, no matter how untimely or unseemly they may be, you are moments from a miracle. Dick's small act of obedience turned into a miraculous moment that quite possibly altered a family tree for generations to come.

Undercover Prophets

I can't imagine Dick Foth ever introducing himself this way: "Hi, I'm Dick. I'm a prophet." Most of us shy away or run away from people who self-identify that way. But when Dick uttered that word of knowledge in the middle of his message, he may as well have donned Elijah's mantle. We mistakenly miscast prophets as idiosyncratic oracles who predict the future, but that isn't the biblical definition or depiction. In New Testament terms, a prophet is simply someone who speaks words of strengthening, comfort, and encouragement as inspired by the Holy Spirit.[6]

When I started pastoring National Community Church as a twenty-six-year-old rookie pastor, Dick and Ruth Foth were part of our original core group of nineteen people. As a seasoned pastor, Dick took me under his wing. He has been more than just a friend and mentor to me. His well-timed words of wisdom have doubled as prophetic words at critical junctures in my life. In fact, they have so profoundly impacted my life that I convinced Dick to coauthor a memoir titled *A Trip around the Sun*.

Jewish philosophers did not believe that the prophetic gift was reserved for a few select individuals. Becoming prophetic was seen as the crowning point of mental and spiritual development—the more you grow spiritually, the more prophetic you become. It's as simple as seeing and seizing God-ordained opportunities to make a difference in someone's life. The right words spoken at the right time can echo for eternity.

The youth leader who saw Donald Miller's writing potential and spoke into his life was a prophet. So was the Bible study teacher who saw my preaching potential. And so are you.

You are more than your professional identity—more than a doctor, more than a coach, more than an administrative assistant. You are an undercover prophet, strategically positioned by God to speak grace and truth. And when you do, it sets the stage for miracles to happen. And it may only take one word of encouragement.

Let me bring it even closer to home.

If you have children, you are more than a parent. You are a prophet to your children. No one knows them, loves them, or believes in them like you do. And it's your job to call out who God has created them to be. That's precisely what Mary did on the third day of a wedding feast. With four words Mary challenged Jesus to step into His destiny, step into His identity:

They have no wine.[7]

The wine running dry in Cana was no accident. It was a divine appointment. Like most miraculous opportunities, it came disguised as a problem. But Mary saw it for what it really was—Jesus' date with destiny.

5

SIX STONE JARS

They have no wine.

John 2:3 ESV

WATER. TWO PARTS hydrogen. One part oxygen.
It's the most basic chemical compound on earth.
It's also the most vital. It covers 71 percent of the planet. It composes 65 percent of your body.[1]

A well-hydrated person with great survival skills can stay alive as long as twelve days without water, but not everybody is Bear Grylls. Most of us wouldn't make it more than two or three days. Yet because it's delivered through pipes to half a dozen different faucets in our first-world homes, we take water for granted. We can even determine its temperature or buy a deluxe showerhead to maximize water pressure. Of course, the tragic reality is that every twenty-one seconds, a child dies from a disease caused by unclean water.[2]

When was the last time you thanked God for good old-fashioned water?

For me, it was on the North Kaibab Trail about two miles from Phantom Ranch on the floor of the Grand Canyon. We had just run out of water, and it was 110 degrees Fahrenheit in the shade! I quickly discovered that dehydration is mentally and physically debilitating. When we finally reached a water supply, I savored every sip. I never knew that something tasteless could taste so good! For the first time in my life, I saw water for what it really was—a miracle. And that's the pattern, isn't it?

We don't appreciate the miracles God consistently does day in and day out. Forgive me for phrasing it this way, but the problem with God is that God is so good at what He does that we take it for granted! What God does best, like keep our planet in orbit, we often appreciate least. But if we learned to recognize the moment-by-moment miracles that are all around us all the time, we would live in wonderment every second of every minute of every day. We'd also crack the joy code. Joy is not getting what you want. It's fully appreciating what you have. And it starts with the basics, like water.

Water has no caloric value, yet it's vital to metabolism. It's flavorless, but nothing tastes better on a hot summer day. Water is the universal solvent. It's fundamental to photosynthesis. It puts out fires. And what else would we swim in?

Like its transparent color hints at, water may be the most transparent miracle of all. It's overlooked and underappreciated by most of us most of the time. But the first miracle isn't turning water into wine. It's water itself. Let's start there.

Degree of Difficulty

The seven miracles in John's Gospel reveal the range of God's power. From our human vantage point, they seem to go from easy to difficult. Or maybe I should say, from impossible to impossibler. And no, that last word doesn't count in Scrabble. Turning water into wine is more than a minor-league magic trick, but it's not as difficult as resuscitating a dead body that has been decomposing for four days! So the miracles seem to get progressively harder, but remember, to the Infinite all finites are equal. There is no easy or difficult, big or small, possible or impossible. To an omnipotent God, there are no degrees of difficulty.

Anything is possible. Nothing is impossible.

When I need a miracle, I have a tendency to pray louder and longer. I sometimes even pray in King James English like a Shakespearean playwright. Or I pull out some of the Greek words I learned in seminary. But God is unimpressed with our theological words and oratorical cadence. He hears our heart more than our words. He responds to faith, not vocabulary.

What Mary *did not do* at the wedding in Cana may be as significant as what she *did do*. She didn't tell Jesus what to do or how to do it. She simply identified the problem and got Jesus involved. "They have no wine."[3]

Mary said so much by saying so little.

Trust isn't measured by word count. In fact, the more trust you have, the fewer words you need. Miracles don't depend upon your ability to articulate the solution to God. There is no abracadabra. You don't need to know what to say. You just need to know where to turn, like Mary did. And if you turn to Jesus, He can turn your situation right side up and right side out. Of course, you don't need to wait until you need a miracle. If you seek Him first, He won't be your last resort.

One God Idea

I don't know the seating arrangement at the wedding in Cana, but Mary made a beeline for Jesus. That's what Steve

Stewart did when he encountered a problem his engineering mind could not solve. Despite zero experience in the field of hydrodynamics, Steve was asked by the Water4 Foundation to try to design a water pump that could work anywhere in the world for less than $50. In Steve's own words, "I didn't know it wasn't possible." And that's when you're halfway to the miracle!

Ten weeks later, after working eighteen-hour days seven days a week, Steve was running out of ideas. Then he stumbled upon a Leonardo da Vinci sketch of a water pump in a book he had purchased ten years earlier while on vacation in Rome. That five-hundred-year-old sketch inspired an idea that led to a breakthrough in design. What makes that discovery miraculous is the relative obscurity of this particular sketch. This was not da Vinci's *Mona Lisa* or *Vitruvian Man*. In fact, despite extensive research, Steve has not been able to find it in any other books or journals. Yet it had been sitting on his shelf for a decade! God set the table for this miracle ten years before Steve even knew he'd need it.[4]

Da Vinci's original design called for a large bellows and animal skins. Steve substituted PVC pipe, a common commodity even in developing countries. Da Vinci's design didn't account for atmospheric pressure, making it impossible to pump beyond thirty feet. Steve's design can pump up to a hundred feet. The cost per pump? Only $17.84. The Access 1.2, named after the then 1.2 billion people who didn't have access to clean drinking water, has been tested up to 3.2 million strokes without failure.[5]

Steve's water pump is more than a good idea. It's a God idea. Of course, some God ideas involve 1,260 hours of research and a random book. Like a fine wine, they have to ferment in the spirit for months or years or even decades before you pop the cork. But one God idea is worth more than a thousand good ideas. Good ideas are good, but God ideas change the course of history. And Steve has done just that. In a sense Steve turned water into water—clean water. And that one God idea has translated into a miracle for millions.

You are one God idea away from changing history.

The key to this kind of miracle is the anointing. It's a mysterious intangible that is difficult to define, but it supernaturally enables us to function beyond our ability. It's ingenious ideas that didn't originate in our cerebral cortex. It's providential timing that results in supernatural synchronicities. It's divine favor that defies human explanation. And the net result is that we become better than our best.

Toward the end of his life, the apostle John referenced this all-encompassing anointing in his first epistle.

His anointing teaches you about all things.[6]

It doesn't matter what you do, God wants to anoint you to do it. The anointing is not just for preachers. It's for politicians and surgeons and entertainers and entrepreneurs and teachers and lawyers and artists. It's for inventors who have no experience in hydrodynamics. It's for cabinetmakers turned Wine Makers. Without it, you'll never turn water into wine. With it, you might just save a million lives or give a million dollars. It's the *it* factor in any endeavor.

On a recent trip to Ethiopia, I met some visionary leaders who are part of the church we helped plant in Addis Ababa in 2005, Beza International Church. A group of leaders within the church is changing the face of their country by falling on their faces before God. I met a woman who plays a pivotal role in the African Union, a doctor who is building a hospital in a rural region of Ethiopia with very primitive health care, and a real estate developer who is designing the first PGA-quality golf course in East Africa. What I discovered during my visit is that these visionary leaders have one thing in common: they all spend one day a week in prayer and fasting. Instead of going in to their offices, they stay in their prayer closets.

How do you get God's anointing?

You simply ask for it.

God wants to give His gifts more than you want to receive them. But you also have to pray through your business plan or game plan or marketing plan. You might even want to fast before performances, before elections, before meetings. And you can't just seek the anointing. You have to seek God. Get into God's Word and God's presence. The closer you get to God, the closer you'll get to His anointing.

Six Stone Jars

In 1934 Ole Kirk Christiansen was a Danish carpenter turned toy maker. The company he created was called LEGO, a word coined from two Danish words meaning "play well." Their motto? *Only the best is the best.* That's not a bad encapsulation of the miracle at Cana. The master of ceremonies put it this way to the bridegroom:

> Everyone serves the good wine first, and when people have drunk freely, then the poor wine. But you have kept the good wine until now.[7]

I'd love to see the sheepish smile on the bridegroom's face. Jesus didn't just help him save face. He helped him put his best foot forward. Jesus didn't just save the day. He made the day. And that's what Jesus does best. He can turn the worst days into the best days! And He always saves the best for last.

The raw material for the first miracle is the most basic building block in nature. It's a profound reminder that God doesn't need much to work with. In fact, He doesn't need anything. His best work is ex nihilo. I suppose Jesus could have started with grapes and miraculously expedited the three-year fermentation process, and that would have qualified as a miracle. But by starting with water, Jesus demonstrated His ability to take the simplest thing on earth and turn it into something even more beautiful, something even more flavorful. And if God can do that with water, what can't He do? The God who spoke every atom into existence is the One who can mutate any molecule. That includes blood cells, brain cells, and cancer cells. Our cells are His LEGOs.

Ole Kirk Christiansen was an audacious dreamer, but I doubt that even Ole could have imagined a flagship store in Times Square or Legoland amusement parks across the country, not to mention a Hollywood blockbuster, video games, and themed LEGO sets that seem to make an appearance at every elementary-age birthday I've ever attended. LEGO's annual production of twenty billion bricks boggles the mind. But it all started with a simple building block.

I recently met one of the masterminds behind the LEGO brand at a gathering of entrepreneurs in Las Vegas. He gave every participant six LEGO bricks that turned into an unforgettable object lesson in ingenuity. He asked us to estimate the total number of unique combinations we could create with those six bricks. I guesstimated a few hundred, leaving me just a few hundred million short of the actual answer. I don't think anybody came anywhere close to the total number of possible permutations: 915,103,765.[8]

Hard to believe, isn't it? In much the same way, we grossly underestimate the God who is able to do immeasurably more than all we can ask or imagine. And maybe that's why Jesus starts His miraculous ministry with H_2O—to show what He can do with next to nothing. The object lesson is far more unforgettable than six LEGO bricks. Start with six stone jars. Add water. Bring them to Jesus. And watch what He can do!

The Fifth Force

Hundreds of chemical compounds float around in red wine, each with its own complex chemical formula. So to say that Jesus turned H_2O into C_2H_5OH via the fermentation formula would be an oversimplification.

The miracle at Cana involved a hundred chemical reactions, the most basic of which is glycolysis. In molecular terms:[9]

$$C_6H_{12}O_6 + 2\ ADP + 2\ P_i + 2\ NAD^+ \rightarrow 2\ CH_3COCOO^- + 2\ ATP + 2\ NADH + 2\ H_2O + 2\ H^+$$

The precise mechanism whereby Jesus turned water into wine is a mystery, and that's what makes it a miracle. But it reveals His mastery and majesty at a molecular level. He is *the* catalyst for any and every transformation, whether it's turning water into wine or sinners into saints.

At last count, there were 10^{82} atoms in the observable universe. And every single one traces its origin back to the four words that spoke them into existence: "Let there be light."[10] God created them and God controls them. He can heal them, multiply them, or curse them. He can restore a withered hand or wither a barren fig tree. It's His call because it's His creation.

Abraham Kuyper, the Dutch theologian and former prime minister of the Netherlands, may have said it best: "There is not a square inch in the whole domain of our human existence over which Christ, who is Sovereign over all, does not cry, 'Mine!'"[11] I would simply substitute "subatomic particle" for "square inch."

All things have been created through him and for him. He is before all things, and in him all things hold together.[12]

Physicists have quantified four fundamental forces: gravitational, electromagnetic, strong nuclear, and weak nuclear. But quantum physics postulates the existence of a mysterious fifth force that governs the other four together. And perhaps they're on to something: God is the gluon that binds subatomic particles together. It's His kinetic energy that animates the water molecule, the wine molecule, and every other molecule in the Milky Way. The catch, of course, is that every atom was affected by the fall of man.

When Adam ate from the tree of the knowledge of good and evil, the law of entropy was introduced into the equation of creation. Metal rusts. Food rots. Muscles atrophy. Cells mutate. Stars collapse. And people die. But there is no atom in your body, or in the universe, that is not subject to God's overriding authority. Not the water in Cana that filled six stone jars at a wedding reception. Not the neurons in the right hemisphere of your brain that spark your imagination. Not the leukocytes in your bloodstream that fight off antigens. Not the hepatocytes in your liver that digest and detoxify. Not the oxytocin in a mother's milk that fosters maternal bonding. Not the sperm cell that miraculously mingles with the egg cell to conceive a human being unlike any other who has ever lived. Not even cells that have been dead and decomposing for four days.

Every double helix is subject to its Intelligent Designer. The One who created the genetic code in the first place can most certainly crack it. But let's not forget that the laws of nature—physical, biological, and astronomical—are miracles in and of themselves. So when God overrides a law of nature that He originally instituted, it's really a miracle within a miracle. We shouldn't just thank Him for instantaneous healing that defies medical protocol. We should also thank Him for the healing properties of our immune system. And while we're at it, we ought to thank Him for medical science as well. It's all of the above.

I'm a lifelong asthmatic, and albuterol has literally saved my life countless times. And while I continue to pray for the elimination of all symptoms via miraculous healing, I will thank God for every other miracle along the way! Even if God chooses not to heal me while on this earth, I'll never be short of breath in heaven. The one who reversed the curse of sin will reverse the curse of asthma, the curse of cancer, and the curse of Alzheimer's disease. Sooner or later, there will be no more pain, no more sickness, and no more death. I'd prefer sooner, but I'll take later. Both are equally miraculous.

Wine into Blood

The first miracle foreshadows the last.

At the wedding in Cana, Jesus turned water into wine. At the Last Supper, Jesus raised a cup of wine and said, "This is my blood of the covenant, which is poured out for many for the forgiveness of sins."[13] On the eve of His crucifixion, Jesus turned an ordinary cup of wine into a bottomless glass of grace. He transformed the fruit of the vine into the agent of forgiveness for every sin ever committed, from Adam to the apocalypse.

Without the shedding of blood, there was no remission of sins in the ancient Jewish sacrificial system.[14] But to reverse the curse once and for all required a sinless sacrifice. So "God made him who had no sin to be sin for us, so that in him we might become the righteousness of God."[15] It's the ultimate transformation. Grace is the solvent that bleaches the crimson stain of sin and washes it white as snow. Make no mistake, that is the greatest miracle of all.

When we commemorate the Last Supper via communion, it's a pilgrimage back to the foot of the cross. It's how we, like Mary, make a beeline to Jesus. We can drink the cup of blessing because He drank the cup of wrath. Jesus drank it to the dregs.[16] We should do no less.

I once visited a winery while driving through the Napa Valley because it seemed like the thing to do. My most poignant memory was watching pseudo-sommeliers swish the wine in their glasses and take the tiniest of sips. That's how some of us sample the grace of God. We drink as though His supply of grace is smaller than the communion cups we use to celebrate it. But you'll never get intoxicated with His love that way. You've got to drink it to the dregs.

Bottoms up!

6

ONE NUDGE

Jesus said to her, "Woman, what does this have to do with me? My hour has not yet come."

John 2:4 ESV

WHEN JESUS TURNED water into wine, He turned a wedding party into His coming out party—the wedding at Cana doubled as His miraculous debut. The bride and groom became extras as Jesus took center stage. But it was a supporting actress who played the key role in this fateful scene. If you read between the lines in John 2, it seems like Mary is pushing her son and Jesus is resisting His mother. She wants Him to take the stage, but Jesus is waiting for His Father's cue. The emotional inflections are as subtle as a slight shift in barometric pressure. But Jesus seems hesitant. The question is, why?

Scholars have debated that question every which way, but here's my take: Mary didn't know that the miracle road was a one-way street to the crossroad called Calvary. Jesus knew full well. He knew that His first miracle would trigger the countdown clock to the crucifixion. And that's part of what makes this first miracle so remarkable. It is the by-product of Jesus trusting someone else's instincts! Mary had a sixth sense that this was His moment. And that is one key to cracking the miracle code.

Nine times out of ten, we miss the miracle that is right at our fingertips simply because we're too close to the situation. We need someone to put a spotlight on something that is in our blind spot. Or put a pointy elbow in our ribs! Most miracles take a nudge. We have to be elbowed out of our assumptions, out of our complacency, out of our fears, or out of our failures. And it helps to have a relationship of trust with the one doing the nudging. I have a hard time trusting fly-by-night personalities, no matter how charismatic they may be. I can't trust them simply because I don't know them and they don't know me. But relational collateral reduces the risk of collateral damage. And no one had more collateral with Jesus than Mary.

Sometimes it's harder to believe God for a miracle for *ourselves* than it is to believe God for a miracle for *others*. So we need to borrow faith from someone else's bank. I'm certainly not suggesting that Jesus didn't believe in Himself, but it was a mother's nudge that was the catalyst for this miracle.

Who do you need to nudge?

Duck Commander

I have a confession to make.

I don't watch much reality television, but I love *Duck Dynasty*. Especially the family prayer around the dinner table at the end of every episode! There is something endearing about the redneck Robertson family. And the success of their company, Duck Commander, and hit TV show, *Duck Dynasty*, is so ludicrous it might qualify as miraculous. But it all traces back to a nudge.

The patriarch of the family, Phil Robertson, was running a commercial fishing operation in northwest Louisiana in the early 1970s. He was living his dream, but he knew it wasn't his calling. That's when he went on a hunting trip with his friend Al Bolen. When a large flock of mallards flew overhead, Phil hit them with a hailing call. Al innocently said, "You didn't call those ducks. You commanded them." That's when the door opened and let the future in.

The idea for Duck Commander was conceived in Phil's spirit in that duck blind outside of Junction City, Arkansas. But it took another nudge from another friend to seal the deal. Baxter Brasher noticed that half the congregation at White's Ferry Road Church would corner Phil after services and ask him endless questions about duck calls. Baxter didn't just encourage Phil to design his own duck call; he used his personal financial statement as collateral to help Phil get a $25,000 loan. When Phil asked him what he wanted in return, Baxter said, "I don't want a dime. I want to know that I helped someone get started."[1]

Who do you need to nudge?

If you seek miracles, you probably won't find them. If you seek God, miracles will find you. But don't forget to nudge a few people along the way!

Nearly every miracle recorded in Scripture involves a supporting cast. The two blind men were operating on the buddy system.[2] The paralytic had four friends drop ship him through a hole in the ceiling.[3] Without those extras, the miracle doesn't go down. And what about the boy with five loaves and two fish? He isn't even named in the credits, but talk about fifteen minutes of fame! He was the supporting actor in one of Jesus' most amazing miracles.[4]

If you want the starring role, you'll miss the miracle. If you're willing to be an ordinary extra, God will do something extraordinary.

Choice Architect

In their brilliant book *Nudge*, authors Richard H. Thaler and Cass R. Sunstein cite some fascinating examples of the way small and seemingly insignificant details can have a major impact on behavior. The men's restrooms at Schiphol Airport in Amsterdam are a good example. When the restroom designer etched the image of a black housefly into each urinal, it reduced spillage by 80 percent. According to Aad Kieboom, the man who came up with the idea, "If a man sees a fly, he aims at it."[5]

Kieboom is what the authors call a *choice architect*. And while we may not think of ourselves in those terms, so are we. In big ways and small ways, we influence each other in subtle and not-so-subtle ways. Something as simple as a smile can charge the emotional atmosphere with positivity. One encouraging word can completely alter a relational dynamic.

In the retail realm, choice architects know that color scheme, spatial layout, and product placement subliminally affect the way we feel, the way we choose, and the way we spend. The volume and rhythm of music will affect how long people shop. The color of a room can manufacture a mood. And different scents affect how much customers will pay for a product.

My favorite study involves movie theaters and the smell of popcorn—one of the most memorable scents because of its complex mixture of twenty-three odor compounds. While a control group watched a movie in an unmanipulated environment, an experimental group watched the same movie in a room flooded with the smell of popcorn. The experimental group accurately retrieved 10 percent, 20 percent, and in some cases 100 percent, more memories than the control group. The researchers concluded that the smell of popcorn is a memory stimulant, a memory steroid. I've joked for years that the smell of popcorn is our incense at National Community Church because we meet in movie theaters. But if this study is accurate, our congregants might just have the best sermon recall of any church in the country!

Is it any coincidence that the same God who designed the olfactory bulb with its innate ability to distinguish between ten thousand different scents also gave Moses a secret and sacred formula for incense?[6] I think not. He knew the incense would imprint the soul and trigger worship every time the Israelites came close enough to the tabernacle to catch wind of it. He also gave them blueprints that included furniture, fixtures, and equipment—right down to the color of the curtains.[7] The Architect of the universe laid out every square inch of the tabernacle so there was a place for everything and everything was in its place.

With that same type of intentionality, God plans our plotline. He orders our footsteps.[8] He prepares good works in advance.[9] And He works all things together for good.[10] God has given us free will, but no one orchestrates opportunities like the Omnipotent One. He provides an entry ramp into every opportunity. He provides an exit ramp out of every temptation. He even stands at the door and knocks.[11] Or He sends someone like Mary to knock on the door of opportunity for Him.

I have no idea what situation you find yourself in, but God has you right where He wants you. Even if it's not where you want to be.

So what are you out of?

Time? Love? Money? Energy?

What has run out in your life that you need God to replenish?

Don't look for the exit before you look for an opportunity. God is setting you up!

Little Nudges

You cannot make choices for others. And if your heart has been broken by an abusive parent or a rebellious child or an ex-spouse, that might be what you need to hear. You shouldn't take responsibility for someone else's sins, but you are able to choose your response. You are, in fact, a choice architect.

If you are in a position of leadership, engineering opportunities is part of your portfolio. It doesn't matter whether you're a parent or a coach or a manager or a pastor. One well-timed compliment can open the door and let the future in. One nudge in the right direction can change a plotline for eternity. You don't need to put undue pressure on yourself—don't worry about missing opportunities or making mistakes. God is the God of second chances, and third and fourth and hundredth. But when the Spirit gives you a nudge, obey it. If you don't, you'll never know where the rabbit hole would have taken you. If you do, the Wild Goose chase begins.[12]

The first key to experiencing the miraculous is discerning those little nudges.

Mary learned to discern the Spirit's nudges as a teenager. And compared to the virginal conception, every other nudge probably seemed pretty tame. When the Spirit nudged her and Joseph to flee to Egypt, they obeyed. The wedding at Cana was no different. Like a parent who has just taken the training wheels off a bike, Mary gives Jesus enough of a push to catapult Him into this miracle.

Hebrews 10:24 tells us:

> Let us consider how we may spur one another on toward love and good deeds.

A spur is an apparatus used to nudge. Sometimes it's a pat on the back. Sometimes it's a kick in the butt. But either way, there is someone in your life who needs a nudge! And it starts with obeying the nudges of the Holy Spirit.

That's what a man named Peter did when he switched planes in Phoenix. He'd been reading a copy of my first book, *In a Pit with a Lion on a Snowy Day*. One sentence pinged him: "God is in the business of strategically positioning us in the right place at the right time, but it's up to us to see and seize those opportunities that are all around us all the time."[13] Peter said hello to the young lady next to him, but she shut him down with one of those looks that says, "Please don't talk to me the rest of the flight, and the armrest belongs to me!" But the Spirit kept elbowing him right in the ribs. Peter was afraid of offending her, but he was more afraid of offending the Holy Spirit. So he leaned over and said, "I know it's absolutely none of my business, but you seem to be carrying a burden. If sharing it with a complete stranger might help, I'm all ears." The seventeen-year-old girl revealed to him that she was three months pregnant and running away from home. Her boyfriend had told her to take off and take care of it, so she stole her dad's credit card and bought a one-way ticket to Vegas to get an abortion. After she shared her story, Peter shared the gospel. When they landed in Vegas, he convinced her to call her parents, who were worried sick. Her parents convinced her to grab the next flight home so they could take care of their daughter and granddaughter.

One life, perhaps two, was saved that day! All because one man knew that a seat assignment might just be a divine assignment. And when we obey those holy nudges, the Grand Master strategically positions His pawns to checkmate the enemy's plans.

The couple who got married at Cana walk off the stage and out of the script of Scripture, but the third day of their wedding feast was undoubtedly the defining moment of their lives. Every time they reminisced about their wedding reception or sipped a glass of wine, it didn't just jog their memory—it jogged their faith. And that's what miracles do. When God does a miracle, the way we steward it is by believing Him for even bigger and better miracles. And we nudge others to do the same!

THE SECOND SIGN

Once more he visited Cana in Galilee, where he had turned the water into wine. And there was a certain royal official whose son lay sick at Capernaum. When this man heard that Jesus had arrived in Galilee from Judea, he went to him and begged him to come and heal his son, who was close to death.

"Unless you people see signs and wonders," Jesus told him, "you will never believe."

The royal official said, "Sir, come down before my child dies."

"Go," Jesus replied, "your son will live."

The man took Jesus at his word and departed. While he was still on the way, his servants met him with the news that his boy was living. When he inquired as to the time when his son got better, they said to him, "Yesterday, at one in the afternoon, the fever left him."

Then the father realized that this was the exact time at which Jesus had said to him, "Your son will live." So he and his whole household believed.

This was the second sign Jesus performed after coming from Judea to Galilee.

John 4:46–54

7

SUPERNATURAL SYNCHRONICITY

There was a certain royal official whose son lay sick at Capernaum.

John 4:46

ON APRIL 14, 1865, President Abraham Lincoln sat in the presidential box at Ford's Theater with his wife, Mary Todd Lincoln, for a Good Friday performance of *Our American Cousin*. General Robert E. Lee had surrendered the cause of the confederacy at Appomattox Court House just five days earlier. Elation was in the air, but a battle-scarred nation would soon experience the same emotional whiplash Jesus' disciples did when they went from the adrenaline rush of the triumphal entry to the gut-wrenching grief of the crucifixion in a week's time.

The renowned actor John Wilkes Booth knew the play by heart, so he waited until Act III, Scene II. That's when seventeen hundred theatergoers would laugh loudly at the funniest line in the script. The president's box was supposed to be guarded by John Frederick Parker, but he left for a local tavern during the second intermission with the president's footman and coachman. When the audience chuckled on cue, the Southern sympathizer, Booth, shot the president at point-blank range in the back of the head.

The president's oldest son, Robert Todd Lincoln, had declined the invitation to attend that evening's production, but he was by his fallen father's side minutes after a messenger delivered the news. Robert would be no stranger to death, having the unfortunate distinction of witnessing two other presidential assassinations. He was serving as secretary of war under President James A. Garfield when Garfield was gunned down by Charles Guiteau at a train station in Washington, DC, on July 2, 1891. The second incident happened at the Pan-American Exposition in Buffalo, New York, on September 6, 1901. Lincoln attended at the invitation of President William McKinley, who was shot by anarchist Leon Czolgosz.

While it seems Robert Todd Lincoln had a knack for being in the wrong place at the wrong time, one such brush with death was far more fortuitous. Just months before his father's assassination, Robert was standing on a train platform in Jersey City, New Jersey. Jostled by the large crowd, he fell off the platform just as a train started moving down the tracks. In a 1909 letter to Richard Watson Gilder, editor of *The Century Magazine*, Lincoln recounted the events of that fateful evening. While he hung helplessly over the train tracks, life in the balance, a bystander seized his collar and pulled him to safety. Lincoln immediately recognized his rescuer as none other than famed actor Edwin Booth, older brother of John Wilkes Booth.[1]

Coincidence or providence?

That's *the* question, isn't it? And not just for history's most improbable concurrences but for our daily happenstance as well. Does God order our footsteps? Even the ones that seem like missteps? Or are we blazing our own trail?

Some would argue the lifesaving effort of Edwin Booth an uncanny coincidence, the by-product of random chance. But if you believe in a Choreographer who sequences every step, there are no coincidences. Only providences. No accidents. Only divine appointments. Every twist of fate is a part of the dance originally designed by God Himself.

Does that mean that God had a hand in the assassination plot of Abraham Lincoln? Absolutely not. John Wilkes Booth pulled the trigger. Then was God missing in action on the night of April 14, 1865? No. The algorithm of the Almighty includes free will. And for better or for worse, free will is the free radical.

Actions and Reactions

My friend Kevin Ramsby is a survivor.

Kevin pastors Revival Tabernacle in downtown Detroit where he's devoted his life to working with gangbangers and drug addicts. That should warrant special protective custody from the Almighty, shouldn't it? But Kevin's dream turned into a nightmare at 3:00 a.m. on August 4, 2009, when he was stabbed thirty-seven times during an armed robbery of his home.

Four feet of scars cover Kevin's body, but his sense of humor survived uninjured. Kevin underwent numerous surgeries after the attack, including emergency surgery to repair ruptured intestines. I've had the same exact surgery, under very different circumstances. So when Kevin and I discovered that both of our belly buttons were in different places post-surgery, we enjoyed a good laugh.

When tragedy strikes, the question that comes to mind is universal: *Where in the world was God?* Kevin wasn't sure until the doctors and investigators shared their reports with him in the aftermath. Half a dozen knife wounds were millimeters away from killing Kevin or paralyzing him for life. That's miracle number one, or numbers one through six. But the police report is even more mysterious and miraculous than the medical report. Investigators found the pool of blood where Kevin lay helplessly at the top of the stairs, as well as bloody prints on the walls of his home. But there was one thing conspicuously missing: there were no bloody footprints between Kevin's home and the neighbor's house where he went for help. Not a single droplet of blood was found. How Kevin got to his neighbor's house is both a mystery and a miracle!

Only God.

At the sentencing of his attacker, Wesley McLemore, Kevin refused to give a victim's statement. He gave a life statement. He did more than proclaim his forgiveness for Wesley. Kevin befriended the man who tried to kill him. Wesley's family and friends have disowned him, but Kevin hasn't. Kevin is Wesley's sole contact outside of prison. In Kevin's words, "God has forgiven me so much, how can I not forgive?"

It's that simple.

It's that difficult.

The true test of our faith is not our actions. It's our reactions. It's relatively easy to act like Jesus. It's much harder to react like Him. And forgiveness is the litmus test.

I promise you this: God did not cause this violent crime. Wesley McLemore made an evil decision, inspired by the evil one who comes to kill, steal, and destroy. But just like Joseph, who was the victim of a violent crime, Kevin experienced a Genesis 50:20 moment. When Joseph was reunited seventeen years later with the brothers who tried to kill him, he didn't give a victim statement. He said:

68

You intended to harm me, but God intended it for good, to accomplish what is now being done, the saving of many lives.[2]

Through Kevin's courage and God's grace, a horrific accident was transformed into a divine appointment for every person on the police force and medical staff who have put their faith in Jesus Christ because of Kevin's crazy forgiveness and, more significantly, the crazy forgiveness of the sinless Son of God.

Accident? Or divine appointment?

It depends on your reaction.

You Go Nowhere by Accident

When I first moved to Washington, DC, I had the privilege of sharing a meal with Senate Chaplain Dr. Richard Halverson. (Part of what made it unforgettable is that the former heavyweight champion of the world, Muhammad Ali, was eating at the table right next to us in the Senate dining room.) Prior to serving the Senate, Dr. Halverson pastored Fourth Presbyterian Church in Bethesda, Maryland, for twenty-three years. He did what pastors do—everything from preaching and counseling to marrying and burying. But he believed his most important function was pronouncing his carefully crafted benediction at the end of every service:

> You go nowhere by accident.
> Wherever you go, God is sending you.
> Wherever you are, God has put you there; He has a
>   purpose in your being there.
> Christ who indwells you has something He wants to
>   do through you where you are.
> Believe this and go in His grace and love and power.[3]

Dr. Halverson reminded his congregation of that simple truth week in and week out until his death on December 1, 1995. Then he reminded them one last time. At the conclusion of his funeral service, Dr. Halverson himself gave the benediction via recording. There wasn't a dry eye in the place!

You go nowhere by accident.

You may not be right where you want to be, but God can use you right there. In fact, God may have you right where He wants you. Whether you're taking a mission trip halfway around the world or a trip to the local grocery store, God is setting up divine appointments along the way. The challenge, of course, is that they are harder to recognize closer to home because we operate on autopilot. Don't be in such a hurry to get where you're going that you miss the miracles along the way—or the miracles that may be out of your way!

The Grand Subplot

In first-century Israel, royal officials and itinerant Jewish rabbis ran in very different social circles. In fact, they avoided each other like the plague. But desperate times call for desperate measures, especially when your son is at the point of death. We will move heaven and Earth if that's what it takes. Or humble ourselves before the Maker of heaven and Earth! The royal official in John 4, who probably reported to Herod himself, defied cultural protocol when he sought an audience with the One rumored to turn water into wine. He subjected himself to someone over whom he had political power. In fact, he knighted Him *Sir* Jesus. That one term of endearment, "sir," may seem like a minor detail, but it's a major deal. I'm quite certain Jesus would not have responded to a plea bargain based on political power. In my experience,

God doesn't respond well to blackmail or bribery. But He will move heaven and Earth to respond to a humble plea for help, even if the request comes from a Roman bureaucrat who belonged to the wrong political party.

The first miracle at Cana was molecular. The catalyst was a chemical reaction that mutated water molecules, revealing His microscopic mastery of subatomic particles. The second miracle is both physiological and geographical. Jesus relieves a dangerously high fever without the aid of acetaminophen. But the key fact is this: Jesus turns down the temperature from twenty miles away! Many of Jesus' miracles happen via the laying on of hands, but this one is a long-distance miracle. The second miracle reveals more than His ability to regulate the hypothalamus, the brain's thermostat. It shows off His *macroscopic* mastery of time and space.

The catalyst for this miracle is a divine appointment between unlikely candidates. I call them supernatural synchronicities. When you meet the *right* person in the *right* place at the *right* time and you have no explanation for how it happened, God might be setting you up. And that is more than a subplot in Scripture. If you live a Spirit-led life, it'll become a subplot in your life as well. You cannot set up supernatural synchronicities. That is God's job. But it's your job to see them and seize them.

Networked

How do you spot supernatural synchronicities? How do you get in on supernatural subplots? What is the cause and effect?

If you want to be on the *effect* side of the miracle equation, a humble plea for help is a good place to start. If you want to be on the *cause* side, treat people the way Jesus did. Deadbolt doors will open sesame. And you won't have to go looking for opportunities. They'll come knocking on your door, just like the royal official.

My friend Justin Mayo is the founder and executive director of an amazing organization called Red Eye. As the name suggests, most of his ministry happens in the wee hours of the morning. Justin has hosted his fair share of after-parties for the who's who of Hollywood, but he is no respecter of persons. He's just as passionate about their Mother's Day makeover party for homeless women living on Skid Row.

Justin is one of the most networked people I've ever met. He has more access than *Access Hollywood*. And I think it's because he's not looking for favors. He's giving them. People feel safe around Justin because he loves them the way Jesus did, with no strings attached. Justin could tell dozens of stories of famous friends he had no business being in the same room with but met because supernatural synchronicities keep happening right and left. From the red carpet to Skid Row, Justin gets in on supernatural subplots simply because he does this: love people when they least expect it and least deserve it.

When the royal official came begging for his son's life, Jesus didn't ask for his tax return first. He didn't ask him to withdraw Roman occupation or change Roman law. He did the man a favor without asking for one in return. That is the catalyst for many a miracle.

Who's Who

In the city where I live, it's all about who you know. Political appointments don't happen because of what you know. Neither do political favors. Your social network is the key card that swipes the door of opportunity. And it wasn't much different two thousand years ago. By virtue of his position, the royal official had access to the who's who of the Roman Empire. And that makes his quest to seek help from Jesus of Nazareth even more remarkable. Remember, in the political sphere, Jesus was subject to the authority of this royal official. But in the spiritual realm, roles are reversed. The authority of the King of Kings trumps the authority of any earthly king. And that's our trump card. Miracles are way beyond our human ability, but they are well within our authority as the children of God.

I was reminded of this during a recent all-night prayer vigil at National Community Church. As our church threw down the prayer gauntlet, I had a distinct impression that 535 8th Street SE was the most important address in the nation's capital during those twelve hours of intercession. I don't mean that in a self-centered, the-world-revolves-around-us kind of way. I honestly don't care if revival starts at NCC or some other church in our city—we just want in on what God does. But that night, I felt like we were at the very epicenter of God's manifest presence. Even 1600 Pennsylvania Avenue had nothing on us. Our church is literally surrounded by places of unparalleled political importance—we sit in the shadow of the White House, the Capitol, and the Supreme Court. But ultimate power is found in the One who sets up and takes down earthly kings. Our authority is far greater in both scope and potency. It's higher and longer and stronger.

My longtime friend and mentor Dick Foth moved to Washington, DC, in 1994 to work with the who's who of Washington. Dick befriended everybody from members of Congress and cabinet members to generals and admirals. Yet despite his credentials as a former college president, Dick was intimidated by Washington's power brokers. He felt like he was out of his element, out of his league. Then he discovered a secret: everybody has an agenda for people in power. So when Dick met these statesmen and told them he didn't want anything from them, he gained incredible spiritual leverage. The defining moment for Dick happened in the Capitol building itself. He heard the still small voice of the Holy Spirit say, "If you speak to the king of the universe in the morning, it's no problem speaking to a United States Senator in the afternoon."

Who is the royal official in your life?
Who is out of your league?
Who do you have no business doing business with?

Don't be intimidated by their power.
You answer to a higher power.

It might seem like they have what you want, but you have what they need. And if you follow Jesus, royal officials will seek an audience with you because you have something to offer that power cannot control and money cannot buy.

Joseph was powerless in prison, but he could do something no one else could. His ability to interpret dreams led to a supernatural synchronicity that saved two nations from famine. God revealed secrets to Joseph that He didn't reveal to anyone else. That is what distinguished Joseph. And that is what will distinguish you.

Six Degrees of Kevin Bacon

In the 1960s, psychologist Stanley Milgram conducted a social experiment that was later popularized by the parlor game "six degrees of Kevin Bacon." Technically known as "the small world phenomenon," the conclusion of Milgram's study was that on average any two people in the United States are separated by only six acquaintances.

Stanley Milgram selected the names of 160 people living in Omaha, Nebraska, and sent them a chain letter in the mail. In the letter was the name of a stockbroker in Boston, Massachusetts. Each person who received the letter was instructed to add his or her name to the chain letter and send it to an acquaintance that he or she thought would get the packet closer to the stockbroker in Boston. They could send it to somebody they knew in Boston, or another stockbroker, or perhaps someone with the same last name as the intended recipient. When the chain letter finally got into the stockbroker's hands, Milgram calculated how many steps it took to get there. On average, it took six relationships or less.

That number very well may have gone down in the last half century because of Facebook and Twitter alone. We are socially connected unlike any generation before us. But even if technology hasn't decreased the six degrees of separation, it has dramatically reduced the real time between us.

Then you add God into the equation.

God knows everybody. Even more, He knows everybody in every way imaginable. He doesn't just know the past. He knows the future. He even knows the number of hairs on our head, pre- and post-shower.

So if you know God, there is only one degree of separation between you and everybody else on the planet. No one is more than one prayer away. God can grant you access to anybody, including Pharaoh. They may even come knocking, like the royal official.

Joshua Dubois recently released a book titled *The President's Devotional*. It contains the daily devotions that Joshua penned for the President of the United States while he led the White House Office of Faith-Based and Neighborhood Partnerships. As his pastor, I'd like to think that a few of my sermons influenced a few of his devotionals. This might be fanciful thinking on my part, but I like to think I had the president's ear a time or two. With Joshua as a middleman, there was only one degree of separation between me and the president of the United States.

You have more access than you realize because you have more authority, as a child of the King, than you could ever imagine. So here's my advice: don't worry about meeting the right person. Meet with God. And God will make sure you meet the right person at the right time.

The church I pastor is made up of mostly single twenty-somethings, so one of our predominant prayers is about finding Mr. or Ms. Right. That's why I often offer the above reminder to overanxious singles. There is nothing wrong with Match. com, but no one can orchestrate a romantic rendezvous like the Matchmaker Himself.

Lord Latitude is His name.

Supernatural synchronicities are His game.

The First Step

One of history's most important synchronicities happens in Acts 8.

God tells Philip to take the desert road south from Jerusalem to Gaza. He doesn't tell him why he's going or what is going to happen once he gets there, but Philip obeys anyway. Honestly, that's where most of us get stuck. We want God to reveal the second step before we take the first, but faith is taking the first step before God reveals the second step! And if you take that step of faith, a divine appointment may be right around the corner. Philip meets an Ethiopian eunuch on the way, interprets a passage of Scripture, shares the gospel, and baptizes him in one fell swoop. Right after this supernatural synchronicity, Philip is instantaneously transported to Azotus, latitude and longitude 31°49'N, 34°35'E. I don't think Philip dematerialized and rematerialized Star Trek style. But one way or the other, the Lord of latitude and longitude pulls off quite the supernatural stunt.

For the record, teleportation is not a spiritual gift. It's a miracle. And while it happens very rarely in Scripture, God is always positioning people in the right place at the right time via the prompting of the Holy Spirit. And if we obey those promptings, like Philip did, we change the course of history.

I've been to Ethiopia multiple times and witnessed first-hand the move of God that is happening there. In 2005, we helped plant Beza International Church in the capital city of Addis Ababa under the leadership of Zeb Mengistu. I believe the next chapter of Ethiopia's history will be its greatest chapter, but the country has a long history of Christianity that traces all the way back to one divine appointment between two people who never should have met. It was the first link in an unbroken chain of Christianity that spans two millennia. And the aftershocks of that one supernatural synchronicity still register on the Richter scale two thousand years later.

Two Sparrows

The last time I checked, the population clock ticked 7,121,929,889. If you managed to line everybody up in a single-file conga line, it would stretch 1,483,735 miles. That's long enough to circle the earth at the equator 59 times, which reminds me of something I've said to my one and only daughter, Summer, since she was a little girl: "If all the girls in the world were lined up, and I could only choose one, I'd choose you." My terms of endearment take on even greater meaning when you consider the actual numbers—I might have to circle the earth quite a few times to find her!

When you consider the vast number of people who inhabit this planet, it's easy to feel insignificant, but it should produce the opposite emotion. You aren't one in a million. You are one in seven billion. Yet Jesus says:

> Are not two sparrows sold for a penny? Yet not one of them will fall to the ground outside your Father's care. And even the very hairs of your head are all numbered. So don't be afraid; you are worth more than many sparrows.[4]

A sparrow was the cheapest ticket item in the food market in ancient Israel. Two sparrows could be purchased for one of the smallest and least valuable coins. Yet not one of them falls outside the Father's care or knowledge or view. Translation: God cares about every minute detail of His creation. Nothing is outside the scope of His care, His concern. Not even the high fever of a royal official's young son living in Capernaum.

One of my favorite commentaries on this verse comes from an unlikely source. Benjamin Franklin alluded to it during a critical moment in American history—the Constitutional Convention on June 28, 1787. After weeks of fruitless debate and frayed emotions, the venerable statesman addressed the convention with these words:

> I have lived, Sir, a long time, and the longer I live, the more convincing proofs I see of this truth—that God governs in the affairs of men. And if a sparrow cannot fall to the ground without his notice, is it probable that an empire can rise without his aid? We have been assured, Sir, in the sacred writings, that "except the Lord build the House, they labor in vain that build it." I firmly believe this.[5]

I firmly believe it as well.

The problem is that children who can't swim fall into pools and drown, innocent people are hit by drunk drivers, and defenseless children are victimized by abusive family members. So how do you juxtapose that with this verse of Scripture?

Why doesn't God cure all cancer, stop all accidents, and end all starvation?

Jesus didn't sidestep these questions. When he encountered a man who was born blind, he dealt with the issue of pain and suffering with grace and truth. We'll do the same when we look at the sixth miracle, but the next paragraph is a placeholder until then.

We live in a fallen world with free will. We know that God loves us and has a wonderful plan for our lives, but we conveniently forget the flip side: the enemy hates us and has a horrible plan for our lives. His agenda is to steal, kill, and destroy.[6] That doesn't mean we should live in fear, because as John reminds us, He that is in us is greater than He that is in the world.[7] And "if God is for us, who can be against us?"[8] But we best not forget that each of us is born on the cosmic battlefield between good and evil. And we must choose sides. In the immortal words of Abraham Lincoln, "My concern is not whether God is on our side; my greatest concern is to be on God's side."[9]

When you choose God's side, it doesn't mean immunity from all sickness or insurance against all accidents. Bad things happen to good people. But reality is redefined by our reactions to those situations.

Consider Nick Vujicic.

Nick was born without arms or legs, but he refuses to be defined by his handicaps. Instead, he defies them. I love the cover of his book, *Unstoppable*. It's a picture of Nick surfing! How is that even possible without legs or arms? But what I love even more is that Nick keeps a pair of shoes in his closet. Stop and think about it. Why would someone without legs need a pair of shoes? In Nick's words, "I keep a pair of shoes in my closet because I believe in miracles."[10]

You cannot control your circumstances, but you can live with holy confidence, knowing that all things work together for good to those that love God and are called according to His purposes.[11] The same God who turned water into wine can turn your pain into someone else's gain, your hurt into someone else's healing, your worst day into your best day.

He did it for Joseph thousands of years ago.

He did it for Kevin a few years ago.

And He can do it for you right here, right now.

8

GOD SPEED

The official said to him, "Sir, come down before my child dies." Jesus said to him, "Go; your son will live." The man believed the word that Jesus spoke to him.

John 4:49–50 ESV

IN THE CRYPT of the Capitol, there hangs a bronze plaque commemorating the inventor of telegraphy, Samuel Morse. When I first saw it, it seemed oddly misplaced. Shouldn't those walls be reserved for politicos? But Morse had a unique symbiosis with the Capitol. Two decades before his history-changing invention, Morse was commissioned to paint *House of Representatives*, a then-famous depiction of a night session of Congress.

In 1825, Morse returned to Washington to paint a portrait of the Marquis de Lafayette, the leading French supporter of the American Revolution. While Morse was painting, a horse messenger delivered a one-line letter from his father:

"Your dear wife is convalescent." By the time Morse arrived in New Haven, Connecticut, his wife had already been buried. Heartbroken by the fact that he was unaware of his wife's failing health and lonely death for more than a week, Morse stopped painting and started pursuing a means of rapid long-distance communication.

The painter-turned-inventor actually set up shop in the Capitol. Morse tested his telegraph prototype by sending messages between the House and Senate wings. According to the Senate doorkeeper, Isaac Bassett, many senators were skeptical, but Morse was able to secure a $30,000 congressional appropriation to build a thirty-eight-mile telegraph line along the Baltimore and Ohio Railway from Washington, DC, to Baltimore.

On May 24, 1844, a large crowd gathered inside the Capitol to witness Morse tap a message in the language he created, Morse code. The message itself was chosen by Annie Ellsworth, daughter of the US Patent Commissioner Henry Leavitt Ellsworth. And while many can recall those infamous words from a high school history class, few know that it's a sacred verse of Scripture. Annie aptly chose Numbers 23:23 in the King James Version, and it did not return void. Moments after the four-word message was received at a railroad depot near Baltimore, the same message was relayed back to the Capitol: "What hath God wrought?"

The Death of Distance

A hundred years ago, information traveled at the speed of ships, trains, and horses. Traveling seventy-five miles a day on horseback, Pony Express riders made the two-thousand-mile trip from Saint Joseph, Missouri, to Sacramento, California, in ten days flat. Tweet that! When George Washington died on December 14, 1799, it took a week for word to travel from Virginia to New York. Many Americans didn't receive the news until the next calendar year.

International news traveled even slower. Newspapers sent reporters to the boat docks to gather news from passengers debarking ocean liners. It may be an urban legend, but King George is purported to have made the following entry in his journal on July 4, 1776: "Nothing much happened today." It's quite possible given the fact that it took several weeks for the news of revolution to cross the pond. Sometimes the slowness at which news traveled had tragic consequences. Two thousand soldiers were killed in the Battle of New Orleans in 1815, two weeks after the relevant peace treaty had been signed in London.

Just a hundred years ago, the American transcontinental phone system had the capacity to handle only three simultaneous calls. We are now Wi-Fied in ways our great-great-grandparents never could have imagined. We are witnessing the virtual death of time and distance. The world keeps getting smaller and smaller, faster and faster.

Against that backdrop, consider the uniqueness of the second miracle. Most of the miracles Jesus performed were in-person encounters—toe-to-toe, hand-to-hand, and face-to-face. But the second miracle redefined reality by defying the four dimensions of space and time. It was a long-distance miracle in real time. A miracle by proxy. Jesus didn't just tap a message in Morse code. He sent healing virtue via sound waves that instantaneously healed the royal official's son who was twenty miles out of earshot.

Most of the eyewitnesses to this miracle knew the entire Torah by memory. I can't help but wonder if Numbers 23:23 fired across the synapses of more than one of them: "*What hath God wrought?*"

Spooky Action at a Distance

In 1964 James Stewart Bell published a groundbreaking paper on the Einstein-Podolsky-Rosen paradox that revolutionized the world of quantum physics. Bell disproved the principle of local causes. This means that regardless of distance, everything in the universe is interconnected. The relationship between particles is not always mediated by local forces. It's mediated by the Fifth Force Himself. The One who instituted the speed of light is able to break it. "With the Lord a day is like a thousand years, and a thousand years are like a day."[1]

One of the reasons we have a hard time believing God for miracles is simply because we think of God as being subject to the laws of nature He created and instituted. We can only be in one place at one time, so it's hard to imagine omnipresence. And the second hand only moves clockwise for us, so it's hard imagining eternity. But the God who designed our universe with four dimensions does not exist within them. We can hardly imagine a fifth dimension, let alone a God who is omnidimensional. But the second miracle hints at His superluminal power.

For centuries, classical physics rested upon the assumption that nothing could travel faster than the speed of light. It was the universal speed limit—186,000 miles per second. Some experiments suggest that if two subatomic particles shoot into space as the result of a subatomic reaction, they always seem to influence each other no matter how far they travel. What happens to one particle happens to the other particle superluminally or faster than the speed of light. There is an indivisible link between particles that defies the four dimensions of time and space. The technical term is instantaneous nonlocality, but I like how Albert Einstein referred to it: "spooky action at a distance."

That's not a bad definition of prayer. It results in spooky action at a distance! It's instantaneous signaling that defies space-time limitations. When we pray, those sound waves exit our four-dimensional world. And almost like firing a bullet up into the air, you never know how or when or where that prayer will reenter the atmosphere. It can be answered half a world away before it even leaves your lips. Or like a time capsule, the answer is sometimes unearthed centuries later. But one thing is certain: our prayers don't have expiration dates. Some of them will be answered long after we are gone. Of course, the God of the second hand can also answer them before we even utter them because time is a two-way street to the Almighty.

There is no past, present, or future.
There is no here or there.

Half a World Away

A number of years ago, I was part of a missions trip to the Galápagos, an archipelago of islands off the coast of Ecuador. We island-hopped for a week, sharing the Good News with islanders who had never heard the gospel before.

Before going, one of our prayers was that God would set up divine appointments. I pray the same prayer during my day-in-and-day-out life, but I double down on mission trips. And God answered those prayers with nothing less than a life-changing, life-saving synchronicity.

On our departure day, we got up early for a forty-five minute bus trip across the island of Santa Cruz to catch an airport ferry to a neighboring island. Only one paved road connected the port city and the ferry, with virtually no civilization in between them. That's why we were surprised to see a hitchhiker by the side of the road in the middle of the island, in the middle of nowhere. If I was behind the wheel, I would have waved and kept on trucking, but our bus driver pulled over and picked up a middle-aged man named Raul. It looked like he had been walking all night and he smelled like it too. It was obvious that he hadn't gotten much sleep the night before.

Raul could have taken a seat anywhere on the bus, but God sat him right next to one of the friendliest and most caring people I know, Adam. He was also one of the few people on our team who spoke fluent Spanish. The reason the seat next to Adam was open is that he would occasionally lay down because of excruciating pain in his back. We wouldn't know it until Adam visited his doctor back in DC, but Adam had a T12 compression fracture from cliff jumping the day before. Yet despite his acute physical pain, Adam empathized with Raul's emotional pain.

In the course of their conversation, Raul told Adam that he had considered committing suicide the day before. He had actually tied cinder blocks around his ankles and planned on drowning himself in the ocean because his wife of thirty years had left him. Adam did more than listen to what Raul said; he understood how he felt. It had been only a few years since Adam's wife of fifteen years had left him and he too was suicidal. Raul asked Adam how he handled the loss of his wife. Adam told him that he turned to Christ and Christ gave him a new life.

Raul told Adam that he felt like God was never there for him, but then he discovered differently on August 12, 2006. God sent a busload of Americans as a divine intervention. God chose Adam for this assignment, and that one divine appointment may have been the whole reason we were there. Who knows, maybe it's the whole reason why Adam learned Spanish. And if it was, it was worth it, because Raul found Jesus on that bus.

Lord Latitude strikes again.

On a human level, there is no way Adam and Raul should have ever met. You cannot manufacture those kinds of meetings. They lived in different countries and spoke different languages. Plus, they were separated by several plane rides, bus rides, and boat rides. But the God who exists outside of our four space-time dimensions knows no spatial or chronological limitations. Setting up a divine appointment in a different hemisphere is as supernaturally simple as setting up a divine appointment with your next-door neighbor.

Someday God is going to pull back the space-time curtain and connect the dots between our prayers and His answers. In my mind's eye, it's a borderless blackboard with so many dotted lines that it looks like a postgraduate class in geometry. Some of those dotted lines will span millennia, like the synchronized prayers of Cornelius and Peter in Acts 10. If you are a Gentile follower of Jesus, your prayer genealogy traces all the way back to a divine appointment between the apostle Peter and the Roman centurion, Cornelius, who was the first non-Jewish convert. Other dotted lines will crisscross our man-made geopolitical borders, like the path of the Ethiopian eunuch who became the first missionary to his homeland. And some dotted lines will cross socio-economic chasms, like the one between Jesus and the royal official. And just like the royal official, we will feel our hearts skip a beat when we see how others' prayers were answered in our lives and how our prayers were answered in others' lives.

The Rest of the Story

Remember the story of Steve Stewart, whose God idea translated into the Access 1.2 water pump? Like many miracles, it involved several supernatural synchronicities that happened simultaneously. Let me connect the dots.

On March 23, 2008, Steve and his family gathered to celebrate Easter. It was a very difficult season for Steve because of a surgery that caused health complications. During the eighteen-month healing process, Steve was determined to make the rest of his life count. On Easter he started to pray, but only one word left his lips: "Lord." It was followed by five minutes of silence, along with a few intermittent tears. Then Steve's son said, "Amen?" In that silence, God spoke loud and clear. Steve prophetically pronounced that they'd always remember that Easter Sunday. What he didn't tell them is that he decided that very day to resign from his job. He had no idea what he would do next, but Steve was determined to make his life count. So the next morning, Steve wrote his letter of resignation and slipped it into the top drawer of his desk. He even circled the date on the calendar that he would offer it to his employer.

On that very same Easter Sunday, Bill Hybels, the pastor of Willow Creek Community Church, shared the story of Dick Greenly, a businessman with a God-sized vision to use his corporate expertise to bring clean water to Africa. After the sermon, someone in the congregation was so stirred that he gave Bill a six-digit donation for "the guy in Oklahoma who wanted to put water wells in developing nations"! Using that seed money, Dick Greenly was challenged to find a water pump that was uniquely suited for these regions, but his efforts failed. In fact, Dick Greenly was ready to call off the search in June of 2008.

On June 13, 2008, one week before Steve's premeditated resignation date, a large water pump broke at the plant where Steve was employed. To assist his production manager in quickly solving the problem, Steve placed a call to the only person he knew who knew anything about water pumps, Dick Greenly. Steve and Dick were old friends, but they hadn't spoken in many years. Steve left a voice mail, but Dick didn't receive it because he was leading a "come to Jesus" meeting with his future board of directors to figure out their path forward, which seemed to be no path!

At one point, Dick sarcastically said they could stop the search and try to design something from scratch. Much to his chagrin, that idea was met with great enthusiasm. After resigning himself to giving it a shot, Dick told his board that he knew of only one man who could do it, an old inventor friend he hadn't heard from in years. On Monday morning, when Dick Greenly went to call Steve Stewart, he discovered he already had a voice mail from Steve! Dick asked Steve to meet him for lunch on Wednesday, June 18. When Dick asked Steve if he had time to design a water pump prototype, Steve revealed that the next day was his last day at his current job. He had circled June 18 several months before, on Easter Sunday. And as they say, the rest is history!

God's timing is impeccable, isn't it?

Miracles rarely happen on our time line. And you can't give God a deadline. But you can trust His timing.

He's never early.

He's never late.

He's right on time, every time.

9

THE SEVENTH HOUR

So he asked them the hour when he began to get better, and
they said to him, "Yesterday at the seventh hour the fever left
him." The father knew that was the hour when Jesus had said
to him, "Your son will live."

John 4:52–53 ESV

IN 1994, TONY Snesko moved from San Diego to Washington,
DC, to fight for a noble cause. Tony was deeply concerned
that innocent children were being introduced to pornography
simply because adult channels were one click away from car-
toon channels, so he authored legislation that would force the
cable industry to fully scramble pornography channels.

As Tony prepared to visit all 435 House offices, he circled
the Capitol in prayer seven times. He even let out a Jericho
shout after the seventh circle. Then Tony started his door-to-
door campaign. Many members applauded his efforts, but he
was told it was too little, too late. The telecommunications
bill he was trying to amend had already gone to markup.

There was no way the chairman of the committee would re-open the bill to include Tony's amendment because it would be reopened to anybody and everybody else's amendment too.

Tony walked out of the 220th congressional office de-pressed and defeated. He was ready to throw in the towel when he had a burning bush moment on the second floor of the Longworth House Office Building. Sitting on a cold marble windowsill that overlooked the Capitol, Tony hung his head in defeat. His inner voice said, *Stop wasting your time and go home to San Diego.* Then he heard the still small voice of the Holy Spirit. He recounts the experience:

> Never before, and never since, has God spoken to me so clearly. While I sat there looking down at the marble-tiled floor, totally dejected, these words were spoken to me as clear as a bell: "Who is doing this—you or Me?" I can't explain how I felt when I heard those words, but I straightened up and responded, "You are, Lord!" Instantly I was filled with more excitement than when I had first begun. At each of the following 215 offices, my presentations were given with renewed faith.[1]

When Tony made his last presentation at the Canon House Office Building, his amendment still seemed like a lost cause. But it's not over till God says it's over. If God has ordained your cause, then the battle belongs to the Lord. It's His vic-tory to win, not yours. Tony continues:

> I am not exaggerating when I tell you this. As my leg crossed the threshold, right when I exited the 435th office, my pager went off. Chairman Dingle had just agreed to allow my amendment to be added to his telecommunications bill.[2]

Sometimes God shows up.
Sometimes God shows off.

Of course, you might have to knock on 435 doors! Or walk twenty miles!

Tony was filled with an electrifying sense of God's impeccable timing, the same rush of adrenaline the royal official must have felt in the aftermath of his miracle. He didn't have a pager, but when he and his servants compared sundials, they realized that the miracle happened the split second Jesus proclaimed the official's son's healing twenty miles away.

Calorie Counter

I've made the twenty-mile drive from Capernaum to Cana, and it's not bad by bus. But when was the last time you walked twenty miles? I live four blocks from my office on Capitol Hill, 437 steps door-to-door. Yet I'm ashamed to admit that I drive it half the time! You may not be as lazy as I am, but twenty miles is still quite a hike. And Capernaum was 700 feet below sea level, so it was an uphill climb all the way to Cana.

Let me translate this miracle into calories.

I'm assuming the royal official didn't miss many meals, given his social status. In fact, he may have had his own personal chef, valet, and butler. So he probably packed some pounds. And because this was a crisis situation, I'm sure it wasn't a slow saunter. He was hustling. Throw in a 5 percent incline one way, and my calorie counter comes up with 7500 calories round-trip. For the sake of comparison, running a marathon at an average burn rate of 100 calories per mile would net 2,620 calories. I once burned more than 12,000 calories hiking Half Dome, and it ranks as one of the most grueling days of my life.

My point? Some miracles take sweat equity. Your effort doesn't make them happen, but your lack of effort can keep them from happening. In the words of Dallas Willard, "Grace is not opposed to effort, it is opposed to earning. Earning is an attitude. Effort is an action."[3] You cannot *earn* a miracle, but *effort* is part of the equation. You may have to hike twenty miles uphill, but your extra effort may be the catalyst for a miracle.

Are you willing to knock on 435 doors? Fill six stone jars? Hike twenty miles uphill?

Most of us follow Jesus to the point of inconvenience, but no further. We're more than willing to follow Jesus as long as it doesn't detour our plans. But it was the willingness to be inconvenienced that defined the Good Samaritan. And that's how he became someone else's miracle. Most miracles don't happen on Main Street. They happen off the beaten path, about twenty miles out of town.

If there is a lesson to be learned from the royal official it's this: *if you want to experience a miracle, sometimes you've got to go way out of your way.* I'm not saying you have to make a pilgrimage to some holy place, but don't wait for the miracle to come to you. Go get it. It's our laziness that keeps many miracles from happening. You've got to go the extra mile. Make every effort to get in close proximity to the healing power of Jesus. That's what the woman with the issue of blood did. She fought through the crowds to touch the hem of His garment.[4] That's what the woman with the alabaster jar of perfume did. She crashed a party at a Pharisee's house.[5] That's what the four friends of an invalid did. They airlifted their friend through a hole in the ceiling.[6]

Sometimes God just wants to see if you're serious!

Are you willing to walk to Cana?

Again and Again

Since writing *The Circle Maker*, I've heard hundreds of testimonies of miraculous answers to prayer. The common denominator among them is perseverance in prayer. Those who got an answer kept circling their Jericho until the walls fell down. They didn't just pray like it depended on God; they also worked like it depended on them. They didn't just dream big; they also prayed hard. Most of them didn't get an answer after their first request, but they kept praying through.

Remember the story of Jesus healing the blind man with mud?[7]

It's one of the most encouraging miracles in the Gospels because it took two attempts. Even Jesus had to pray more than once! The first prayer resulted in a partial miracle, but Jesus wasn't satisfied with 20/80 or 20/40 vision. So He doubled back and prayed a second time for a 20/20 miracle: "Then Jesus laid hands on his eyes again."[8]

The operative word is *again*. What do you need to pray for again? And again and again and again? Some miracles happen in stages—even healing miracles. If you get partial healing or partial relief, praise God for it. But don't settle for half a miracle! Keep praying for the whole miracle to happen. Sometimes we let fear keep us from praying for a miracle because we feel like we will have failed if God doesn't answer the way we want. That isn't failure because the answer isn't up to us. The only way we can fail is failing to ask.

I've lost count of how many times I've asked God to heal my asthma. It has not happened, but does that mean I quit asking? I've resigned myself to the simple fact that healing is in God's hands. That's His job, not mine. My job is to keep on asking. After all, God won't answer 100 percent of the prayers we don't pray.

On a recent trip to Israel, I visited the synagogue in Capernaum where Jesus performed multiple miracles. We actually held a healing service right there, and I felt prompted to pray for healing once again. If I was writing the script, I can't think of a more dramatic way of finally answering my lifelong prayer. But the healing didn't happen. I definitely felt a twinge of disappointment when I had to take my inhaler later that day, but I'm going to continue asking. When and where and how God decides to answer is His call. I might not experience healing on this side of heaven, but as long as God gives me breath to breathe, I'll keep asking.

350 Circles

As a pastor and an author, I receive more prayer requests than I can keep track of, but I try my best to honor every single one. Some of them represent more suffering than I can even imagine. I just sit at my desk and cry over them. Others pull my heartstrings because I can identify with the request. One of those requests came from a friend whose friend's son needed a lifesaving kidney transplant.

The transplant was scheduled to take place at Baptist Hospital in Oklahoma City on February 11, 2013. Just a month before the lifesaving transplant, doctors informed family and friends that Marquise no longer qualified for the experimental procedure and his transplant was canceled. It was a bitter pill to swallow, but that devastating news actually steeled their determination.

The kidney donor, Paul Anderson, received a copy of *The Circle Maker* two days after the canceled procedure. He read through the night, finishing the book the next morning. That's when he started circling Baptist Hospital. Over the course of 160 days, Paul circled that hospital like it was Jericho itself. He logged more than 350 miles while circling the hospital 350 times! That's the equivalent of fifteen trips between Capernaum and Cana.

On June 17, 2013, Paul got his answer and Marquise got Paul's kidney.

Now here's the rest of the story.

More than a decade before, Marquise's father, Jim, shared his testimony at a men's retreat at Roman Nose State Park. One of the attendees, Paul Anderson, had no idea what he was doing there. His life was a train wreck. Paul was as far from God as you can get, but Jim's words struck the right chord at the right time.

Jim's words saved Paul's life. Thirteen years later, Paul's kidney would save Jim's son's life.

Like the royal official who walked all the way to Cana, Paul walked around Baptist Hospital. At an average rate of 3 miles per hour, Paul burned approximately 125 calories per lap. Multiplied by 350 round trips, that's a total of 43,750 calories!

In God's kingdom, what goes around comes around. And if you keep praying again and again, your life will turn into a merry-go-round of miracles.

Back to Cana

My first visit to Disney World in Orlando, Florida, ranks as one of the most memorable moments of my childhood. It's not called the Magic Kingdom for nothing. It's like there is pixie dust in the air—it's the most magical place on earth. And whenever you return, the memories and emotions multiply like compound interest. Cana had that same quality to it. Maybe that's why Jesus keeps going back.

Once more he visited Cana.[9]

The second miracle happened within a stone's throw of the first miracle. And I don't think it's coincidental. Miracles often occur in space-time clusters. There are set seasons and specific places where God seems to manifest His presence in unprecedented ways. Cana was one of them. It was hard not to have faith in Cana because the aroma of fine wine was still in the air. I doubt they drank all 757 bottles Jesus had miraculously manufactured at the wedding feast. Some of those bottles became vintage collector's items—spiritual mementos of the first miracle Jesus had done there. And whenever they uncorked a bottle, the aftertaste was pure faith.

There are places where it's hard not to have faith. That's why I pray on the rooftop of Ebenezer's coffeehouse. I have a little more faith when I'm pacing back and forth on top of a miracle God has already done—turning a crack house into a coffeehouse that has served more than a million customers and given away nearly $1 million in net profits. It helps me believe God for even bigger and better miracles because I'm standing on the shoulders of a miracle God has already done.

Do you think David ever went back to the Valley of Elah where he dropped Goliath with a single stone? Did Moses ever retrace his steps to the burning bush? Did Peter ever row out on the Sea of Galilee to the spot where he walked on water? Did Lazarus ever put fresh flowers on the grave where he lay dead for four days?

When we forget the faithfulness of God, we lose faith. That's why we need to go back to the vintage miracles God has already done in our lives.

When you lose your way or lose your faith, you need to go back to the burning bushes in your life.

Go back to the second floor of the Longworth House Office Building.

Go back to Baptist Hospital.

Go back to Cana.

THE THIRD SIGN

Some time later, Jesus went up to Jerusalem for one of the Jewish festivals. Now there is in Jerusalem near the Sheep Gate a pool, which in Aramaic is called Bethesda and which is surrounded by five covered colonnades. Here a great number of disabled people used to lie—the blind, the lame, the paralyzed. One who was there had been an invalid for thirty-eight years. When Jesus saw him lying there and learned that he had been in this condition for a long time, he asked him, "Do you want to get well?"

"Sir," the invalid replied, "I have no one to help me into the pool when the water is stirred. While I am trying to get in, someone else goes down ahead of me."

Then Jesus said to him, "Get up! Pick up your mat and walk." At once the man was cured; he picked up his mat and walked.

John 5:1–9

10

VERY SUPERSTITIOUS

Sir, I have no one to put me into the pool when the water is stirred up, and while I am going another steps down before me.

John 5:7 ESV

IN 1939, GEORGE Dantzig enrolled as a graduate student at University of California, Berkeley, studying statistics under Polish-born professor Jerzy Neyman. At the beginning of one class session, Dr. Neyman chalked two examples of famously unsolvable problems on the blackboard. George happened to arrive late to class that day, missing the disclaimer. He mistakenly thought the unsolvable problems were their homework assignment, so he transcribed them in his notebook and went to work. It took a little longer than he anticipated, but George Dantzig ultimately solved both of them. On a Sunday morning six weeks later, an ecstatic Dr. Neyman knocked on George's front door to share the news. A bewildered George actually apologized, thinking the assignment was overdue.

That's when Dr. Neyman informed George that he had solved two of statistics' unsolvable problems.[1]

With the outbreak of World War II, George Dantzig took a leave of absence from Berkeley to serve the United States Air Force as civilian head of the combat analysis branch. After finishing his doctorate in 1946, George returned to Washington, DC, where he worked as a mathematical adviser to the Defense Department. Then in 1966, George joined the faculty of Stanford University as professor of operations research and computer science. Dr. George Dantzig received numerous awards during his distinguished career, including the National Medal of Science in 1975. For his groundbreaking research in linear programming, the Mathematical Programming Society established the George B. Dantzig award in 1982. The tools Dantzig developed have shaped the way airlines schedule their fleets, shipping companies deploy their trucks, oil companies run their refineries, and businesses manage their revenue projections. Dantzig's legacy is felt far and wide, but the genesis of his genius can be traced back to one seminal moment as a statistics student. In his own words, "If someone had told me they were two famous unsolved problems, I probably wouldn't have even tried to solve them."[2]

We make far too many false assumptions about what *is* and what *isn't* possible. George Dantzig solved those unsolvable problems because he didn't know it couldn't be done. And therein lies one of the secrets to experiencing the miraculous.

Jesus said, "With God all things are possible."[3] And just to make sure we don't miss the point, it's inverted in Luke 1:37: "Nothing is impossible with God" (ESV). Whenever the Bible says the same thing two ways, it's doubly important. The word *impossible* does not belong in our vocabulary. In God's ears, it's an expletive. And it's the primary reason we don't experience the miraculous. We let our logical assumptions trump our theological beliefs. And before we know it, our reality is defined by human assumptions rather than divine revelation. So let me double back to this simple truth: Jesus can make your impossible possible!

Experiencing the miraculous is certainly more than the power of positive thinking. *I think I can, I think I can, I think I can* doesn't always get the train up the tracks like the Little Engine That Could. And it's certainly not some Jedi mind trick. But I do think Henry Ford was right: "Whether you think you can or think you can't—you're right." It's not mind over matter. It's faith over matter.

Faith doesn't ignore a doctor's diagnosis.

It does, however, seek a second opinion from the Great Physician.

A Second Opinion

"You'll never walk again."

Those words echoed in his mind's ear for thirty-eight years.

Scripture doesn't reveal how it happened—whether it was a birth defect or genetic condition or freak accident. But the invalid hadn't stood on his own two feet in nearly four decades!

That's a long time by any measure, but it must have seemed even longer two thousand years ago when the average life expectancy was twenty-eight. That average is skewed by infant mortality rates in the ancient world, but even if you lived past your second birthday, the average only rose to forty. My point? The invalid was way past his prime. In fact, he was living on borrowed time. And I wonder if that's why Jesus singled him out. The man had been sitting by the pool of Bethesda longer than anyone could remember, but what a way for Jesus to prove that His power knows no logical or chronological limits. It's never too late when you turn to the One who can turn back time!

The invalid was out of referrals. His condition was incurable and his case was unsolvable. But that's the Great Physician's specialty. In the face of every diagnosis the invalid had ever been given, Jesus gives a simple prescription:

Get up! Pick up your mat and walk.[4]

Have you ever watched a baby attempt to walk?

It is one of life's simplest and greatest joys—especially for parents. But let's be honest, it's not pretty. Watching a baby take his or her first steps is like watching a drunken sailor walk the plank. They weeble and wobble like nobody's business. In my mind's eye, that's how I see this miraculous scene playing out in John's Gospel. The invalid is no model strutting down the catwalk. This is physical comedy at its finest. The invalid is falling all over himself at first. Those who witnessed it were laughing so hard they were crying. But those tears of laughter turned into tears of joy as they watched this disabled man do something he hadn't done in decades—jump for joy like a little child.

It doesn't matter how bad the diagnosis is or how long you've had the handicap. It's never too late to be who you might have been. If you're breathing, it means God's not finished with you yet. You are never past your prime. But if you want a second chance, you need to seek a second opinion—God's opinion.

God's Got This

When Ethan was in kindergarten, a standard hearing test revealed that he had profound hearing loss in his right ear. A follow-up visit to the ear, nose, and throat specialist further revealed that his right eardrum had actually ruptured. Then a trip to Children's Hospital of Philadelphia resulted in an even more devastating diagnosis—cholesteatoma, a destructive and aggressive growth in the middle ear that would require surgery.

On June 10, 2011, Ethan underwent a seven-hour surgery to remove it. That's when doctors discovered that the growth had completely eroded his eardrum, the bones inside the eardrum, and the ear canal. It was dangerously close to crossing the brain lining. Despite half a dozen surgeries in the span of two years, doctors concluded that his condition would require a more radical craniotomy. The thought of doctors doing open-skull surgery on their son drove Jason and Amy to their knees. But instead of allowing each surgery to shake their faith, they kept falling on their faces and crying out for mercy.

One day Amy was reading a daily devotional, *Jesus Calling*, when Ethan walked into her bedroom and asked her what it said on his birthday. Amy flipped to August 20 and read these words: "I am the God who heals. I heal broken bodies, broken minds, broken hearts, broken lives, and broken relationships. My very Presence has immense healing powers. You cannot live close to Me without experiencing some degree of healing."[5] Amy started crying the second she read it. She felt like that promise was for her, so she started circling it in prayer. By faith, Amy said to Ethan, "I believe God is telling us that He's going to heal you." She asked Ethan if he thought God would do it, and eight-year-old Ethan said, "A man can only hope!"

From that moment on, Amy's mantra was: *God's got this!*

Amy and Jason, along with their church family, started circling Ethan in prayer. Then on June 7, 2013, Ethan was rolled into the operating room. During the scheduled four-hour surgery, it was standard operating procedure for a nurse to provide updates to the family every forty-five minutes. And Ethan's nurse did just that during pre-op, but then the updates mysteriously stopped. By the sixth hour, Amy and Jason were getting nervous. When the nurse finally emerged from the operating room, she told them that the doctor wasn't giving her any information at that point. It wasn't until seven hours after Ethan was wheeled into surgery that a stupefied surgeon informed the family that there was no physical evidence of the disease. The CT scan prior to surgery was completely different from the CT scan they had done a few months before. The cholesteatoma was nowhere to be found, and the parts of the inner ear that had been completely eroded by the disease were completely regenerated. The doctor scratched his head and said there was no explanation for it. In Amy's words:

> To say I was in shock would be an understatement. We looked at each other in utter amazement. We prayed for this—hard— but we were still surprised when God answered those prayers. From what all the doctors tell us, this isn't even possible. Skull bone doesn't restore itself, and cholesteatoma cannot go away on its own. It's just not physically possible. But it's God-possible.[6]

God's got this!

Keep Swinging

For every story of a miraculous healing like Ethan's, there are a dozen stories that don't turn out that way. Healing is the exception, not the rule. And I'll deal with the exceptions when we look at the sixth miracle—the man born blind. But let me share a rule of thumb for now: God won't answer

100 percent of the prayers you don't pray. If you assume the answer is no, you don't even give God a chance to say yes.

Imagine a major league baseball player refusing to get into the batter's box because he doesn't get a hit every time up. Yet that's how many of us approach prayer. We let a few strikeouts keep us from swinging for the fences! Trust me, my prayer batting average is no better than anyone else's. I swing and miss all the time, but if I'm going down, I'm going down swinging.

Ty Cobb, one of baseball's all-time great hitters, had a lifetime batting average of .367. When he was in his seventies, Cobb participated in an old-timers game and a reporter purportedly asked him, "What do you think you'd hit if you were playing major league baseball today?"

Cobb said, "About .310, maybe .315."

The reporter surmised, "That's because of travel, night games, artificial turf, and new pitches like the slider, right?"

Cobb said, "No. I'd only hit .300 because I'm seventy-two years old."[7]

I love that mindset.

Great hitters have short memories, selective memories. So do those with great faith. No matter how many times you strike out, faith keeps swinging for the fences. If you want to experience the miraculous, you have to come to terms with the fact that who, what, when, where, and how aren't up to you. You cannot answer your own prayers. But if you fail to ask God, He cannot answer them either!

When I survey Scripture, it seems to me that most miracles happen to the people who make the fewest assumptions. Joshua did not assume that the sun could not stand still.[8] Elisha did not assume that iron ax heads don't float.[9] Mary did not assume that virgins don't get pregnant.[10] Peter did not assume that he could not walk on water.[11] And Jesus did not assume that death was the end of life.[12]

As you grow more and more in faith, you make fewer and fewer assumptions!

The Wrong Miracle

When I was in the eighth grade, a visitation team from Calvary Church in Naperville, Illinois, came knocking on our front door. We were new to the church, and they wanted to know if there was anything about which we could "agree in prayer." I had a chronic case of asthma that had resulted in half a dozen hospitalizations throughout my childhood, so we asked them to pray that God would heal me.

Several decades later, I still have asthma. But something unforgettable happened that night. When I woke up the next morning, all the warts on my feet were completely gone! I kid you not. My first thought was that there must have been some sort of confusion between here and heaven because I definitely didn't get what I ordered. And that's when I heard the inaudible yet unmistakable voice of God for the first time in my life: "I just wanted you to know that I am able."

God is able.

That's my only assumption.
And any other assumption is a false assumption.
He is the God who can make the impossible possible.

I don't hear the voice of God as often or as clearly as I would like. And guessing the will of God can feel like a game of pin the tail on the donkey. But it is difficult to doubt after an experience like that. God doesn't always answer my prayers how I want or when I want, but I live with an unshakable conviction that God is able.

Five Fingers

The last time our family was in Ethiopia, my friend Zeb Mengistu told us about a recent flurry of healing miracles. One of the disjointing things about visiting a country like Ethiopia is the number of people with very visible physical deformities. And the most obvious reason is that they don't have surgical solutions for their problems like we do in the United States.

The physical needs are very similar, in size and scope, to the ones Jesus would have encountered two thousand years ago. And maybe that's why physical healing is more common in third world countries than first world countries. Of course, it might have something to do with the fact that they have more faith and make fewer assumptions. They don't know what God can't do!

During our visit, Pastor Zeb shared about one of the documented healings. A boy with no fingers on one hand was brought to a healing service. His hand literally had five stubs, but that didn't deter them from praying for him. The pastor who was leading the service prayed for the boy, then turned around and walked away. That's when he heard a pop, followed by another and another and another and another. The crowd started cheering as they saw five new fingers pop out of the boy's hand.

Why don't we witness miracles like that?

One simple answer is the false assumption that they won't happen or can't happen! We don't have the faith to even ask, so we can count these kinds of miracles on one hand. But if we had more faith, we might see a few more miracles of biblical proportions! Like Nick Vujicic, we need to keep a pair of shoes in our closet. Or in this instance, a pair of gloves!

False Assumptions

Modern archaeological excavations have uncovered what is believed to be the ancient pool of Bethesda. Located near the Sheep Gate, the two-pool complex was twenty feet deep and as large as a football field. Surrounded by five roofed colonnades that provided shade from the Middle Eastern sun, it was a natural gathering place in first-century Israel.

For thirty-eight years, a handicapped parking permit hung in the invalid's window. He had a reserved spot at the pool of Bethesda. Day in and day out, he begged for money from bathers. It was rare that they made eye contact with him, even rarer that they gave him a handout. But one thing kept him coming back; one thing kept his hopes alive. Every once in a blue moon, the waters would be stirred. The cause of the stirring was undoubtedly the intermittent springs that fed the pool, but a superstition grew up around the stirring. Some believed that the stirring was caused by angels. And the first one into the water after the water was stirred was the winner, winner, chicken dinner!

Like a bad scene from a tragicomedy, hundreds of invalids would creep and crawl and claw their way to the water, hoping they'd be the first ones there. But the true tragedy was that it wasn't even true! It didn't matter whether they were first or last. It was false hope based on a false assumption. And while it's easy to be dismissive of such silly superstitions, we all know someone who wears their lucky socks on game day, plays the lottery on their birthday, and is very cautious about making plans on Friday the 13th. We all have our pet superstitions. And while those superstitions may seem to invoke the supernatural, they actually revoke it. Anything less than 100 percent reliance upon the miraculous power of God and God alone actually short-circuits the supernatural.

The opposite of belief isn't just unbelief.

It's false belief.

The invalid's greatest handicap wasn't physical. His most debilitating handicap was mental—a false assumption that he needed to be the first one into the pool of Bethesda when the water was stirred. And we make the same mistake, don't we? We keep trying what isn't working. What we need is someone to get in our face and ask us: *How's that working for you?*

If you want God to do a new thing, you can't keep doing the same old thing. If you want to experience the miraculous, you need to unlearn every assumption you've ever made, save one.

God is able.

11

SELF-FULFILLING PROPHECIES

Do you want to get well?
John 5:6

IN NOVEMBER OF 2004, a group of elite medical researchers and practitioners convened for a closed-door conference at Rockefeller University in New York City. The goal of the gathering was to get the most brilliant thinkers in the world in one room trying to tackle the health care crisis, but the outcome was simultaneously encouraging and discouraging. It was encouraging because most health problems are *not* caused by factors beyond our control. And it was discouraging for the very same reason! The experts concluded that they could not fix our problems for us. Only we can fix them ourselves. Unfortunately, we choose not to. Study after medical study identifies five behavioral issues that cause 80 percent of health problems: too much eating, drinking, smoking, and stress, and not enough exercise.[1]

It's that simple.

It's that difficult.

With a few minor changes, we could solve most of our major health problems. But we don't want to. And I don't mean want as in *wish* or *whim*. Every single one of us would wish our problems away on a whim. But it takes more than a wish or a whim to experience lasting change. Here's my working definition of *want*: the sanctified desire and matching discipline to do what needs to be done, no matter how hard it is or how long it takes. No matter what goal you're trying to achieve or problem you're trying to solve, you have to *want it* more than the pain that will be inflicted upon you in the process of trying to attain it.

That's where nine out of ten of us fall short, according to Dr. Edward Miller, the thirteenth dean of the Johns Hopkins University School of Medicine. More than one and a half million Americans undergo a coronary bypass graft every year. And while angioplasty effectively relieves many of the symptoms of clogged arteries, it's a temporary fix. Without a change in eating and exercise habits, the health benefits are short-lived. And patients are told that point-blank. Yet, Dr. Miller notes, "If you look at people after coronary-artery bypass graft two years later, 90 percent of them have not changed their lifestyle."[2]

I daresay every single one of them wants to live, but not enough to change. If the numbers are right, nine out of ten people would rather die than change! And Jesus knew it long before there was a study purporting it.

Point-Blank

The ability of Jesus to formulate the right question at the right time is nothing short of art. He could have schooled

Socrates in the Socratic method. And He would have been unbeatable at twenty questions! Of course, the ability to read minds, which He put on display a time or two, was an unfair advantage.

The Gospels record 183 or so questions, depending on your translation of choice. While they fall into a wide variety of categories, some of the most poignant are the point-blank questions. And one of them is the catalyst for the third miracle. Jesus asks an invalid:

Do you want to get well?[3]

On one level, the question seems a little unkind, doesn't it? Like adding insult to injury. Of course he wants to get well! But that is not an assumption Jesus made. He knew better. You cannot help someone who doesn't want help, no matter how badly they need it. The thief on the cross, the one who hurled insults, is a case in point. He was six feet from salvation, but he cursed the only One who could have helped him.[4]

Over the years, I've cultivated friendships with quite a few people who live on the streets of Washington, DC. I've done more than give them a few dollars here and there. We've shared meals. We've shared stories. And one of the painful truths I've come to realize is that some people want help while others don't. And it's not just those who live on the streets. You cannot help those who won't help themselves, no matter who they are. Some of my homeless friends have gotten homes and gotten jobs. In fact, one of them helps lead our homeless ministry at National Community Church. But for every success story, there are some who resist change, even change for the better. They'd rather live on welfare than get a job, get a home, and get well.

It's easy to become accustomed to our crutches, isn't it? Or in the case of the invalid, adjusted to our two-foot-by-four-foot mat. The invalid's world consisted of eight square feet. He went through the same routine day after day after day. And while that might seem monotonous to us, it was also safe. In fact, his mat may have been his security blanket. But if you want to get well, you can't keep sitting on your security blanket. You can't keep doing the same thing, going to the same places, or hanging with the same people. You've got to get rid of your mat—roll it up and throw it away.

Do you want to get well?

This question gets to some deep-seated issues. For the invalid, getting well meant getting a job. It meant actually using his healed legs. It meant a new level of responsibility to society. Like every blessing from God, it comes with the burden of responsibility to steward it.

Tough Love

Sometimes we need someone to silly-slap us! It might injure our ego, but if the truth is spoken in love, it can heal our soul.

That's exactly what a twenty-two-year-old intern did with me early on in my pastoral ministry. He confronted the pride he detected. Part of me wanted to quickly point out what was wrong with him! How dare an intern indict my integrity? The problem was, he was right. I didn't like it when he said it, but I look back on that awkward moment as a defining moment for me. And I have the utmost respect for that intern and everyone else who has had the courage to challenge me over the years.

In my experience, the best friends ask the toughest questions. And by tough questions, I mean tough love! In the words of Proverbs 27:6, "Faithful are the wounds of a friend; profuse are the kisses of an enemy" (ESV). Don't surround yourself with people who kiss up or suck up. You need some people in your life who will get in your face, get in your business!

Do you want to get well?

If you do, then you need to hear what you don't want to hear and do what you don't want to do. You can't expect God to do the supernatural if you aren't even willing to do the natural. You've got to do your part so God can do His part. Like the invalid, you have to be willing to carry your weight. Only God can perform miracles, but there is almost always a human element involved.

Remember, Naaman had to dip in the Jordan River seven times.[5] The woman with the issue of blood had to fight through the crowds to get close enough to Jesus to touch the hem of His garment.[6] And the disciples had to haul in their nets and cast them on the other side of the boat.[7]

Some miracles take tough love.

Some miracles take time.

Some miracles take extra effort.

Some miracles take blood, sweat, and tears.

Atrophy

During my college basketball career, I had reconstructive surgery for a torn ACL in both of my knees. The most painful moment was getting out of bed for the first time after surgery. Have you ever had blood rush to one of your extremities after it's been elevated or the circulation has been cut off? The pain was so acute I almost passed out. Now imagine the invalid standing to his feet after thirty-eight years of being off of them. It wasn't just a rush of adrenaline. It was a blood rush.

While the ligament graft in my knee healed in a matter of months, it took me much longer to regain the muscles that had atrophied. If you've ever been on bed rest or in a cast, you know what I'm talking about. It takes ages to build muscle, but it takes no time to lose it. I actually wore an electrical stimulation device post-surgery to elicit muscle contractions via electrical impulses. The invalid did not have one of those! His legs were skin and bones. He had no muscle. And more significantly, he had no muscle memory!

We take walking for granted, but it's quite the neuro-musculoskeletal feat. Simply standing still requires marvelous coordination between highly sophisticated sensory systems— the small structures in the inner ear regulate balance, the proprioceptors in the joints detect small shifts in alignment, and our eyes provide visual information about the body's orientation in space.[8] So standing still is no simple feat, but ambulation is even more amazing.

When you walk, you function as an inverted pendulum. The kinetic energy of motion—Mass x Velocity^2 ÷ 2—is transformed into gravitational potential energy—Mass x Gravity x Height. If you were a perfect pendulum, you'd convert kinetic energy into potential energy and back without wasting a calorie. But we're only 65 percent of a perfect pendulum, which means that 35 percent of the energy for each step is supplied by the calories we burn. Birds and fish are far more efficient, even though they fly through the air and swim through the water. But that doesn't mean walking is any less miraculous than flying or swimming, especially if you haven't done it in thirty-eight years! In my humble opinion, the invalid walking on land is no less miraculous than Jesus walking on water.

The Law of Requisite Variety

When Jesus told the invalid to get up and walk, He was asking him to do something he hadn't done in thirty-eight years.

And that's what it takes if you want to experience the miraculous. You can't keep doing what you've always done! In fact, you might have to do something you haven't done in a long, long time!

If you want to change, you have to change the equation of your life by adding or subtracting something. You have to do something less, do something more, or do something different.

According to the law of requisite variety, the survival of any system depends on its capacity to cultivate variety in its internal structures. In other words, you have to keep changing. Prolonged equilibrium dulls our senses, numbs our minds, and atrophies our muscles. Your world gets smaller and smaller until your universe is about eight square feet.

Equilibrium is bad.
Disequilibrium is good.

In the realm of exercise, routines eventually become counterproductive. If you exercise the same muscles the same way every time, your muscles start adapting and stop growing. The net benefit decreases. What you need to do is disorient them. And the same is true spiritually.

Routine is one key to spiritual growth. We call these patterns spiritual disciplines. But when the routine becomes routine, you have to change the routine. If you want to get out of a spiritual slump, you need to change something up.

Volunteer at a local homeless shelter or nursing home.
Start keeping a gratitude journal.
Take a personal retreat.
Pick up a different translation of the Bible.
Do a ten-day fruit and vegetable fast like Daniel.[9]

Those small changes in routine can make a radical difference. But it always starts with the first step of faith. The first step is always the longest and hardest, but that one small step often turns into a giant leap.

Self-Fulfilling Prophecies

The fact that the invalid is called *invalid* is no insignificant detail. It'd be like me introducing myself as *asthmatic*. I realize it's a grammatical mechanism used throughout Scripture with a wide variety of nameless people—the prostitute with the alabaster jar, the man born blind, and the woman caught in the act of adultery, to name a few. They are synonymous with their sin, with their sickness. But there is a lesson to be learned: *don't let what's wrong with you define you.* That's not who you are. When my children lie to me, I don't call them liars. I remind them that that's not who they are. I certainly call it what it is—a lie. But I don't let what they've done wrong define their identity or destiny.

Our culture has a tendency to reduce people to labels. Not only is that unhealthy and unholy, it's also dehumanizing. Don't let anyone label you besides the One who made you. Take your cues from Scripture.

You are *more than a conqueror*.[10]
You are *the apple of God's eye*.[11]
You are *sought after*.[12]
You are *a joint heir with Christ*.[13]
You are *a child of God*.[14]

If you look up *impetuous* in the dictionary, there should be a picture of Peter. He was absolutely unreliable! Yet Jesus gives him a new label—"The Rock."[15] Seems like a misnomer, doesn't it? Nothing could have been further from the truth, but Jesus redefines Peter's identity and forecasts his future with one new label. And Peter ultimately lived up to his new name.

That's the power of a prophetic word.

Our words are far more powerful than we realize.

In 1963, Hall of Fame baseball pitcher Gaylord Perry made an offhanded comment before stepping into the batter's box: "They'll put a man on the moon before I hit a home run." That statement wasn't totally baseless, given the fact that most pitchers aren't great hitters. But it's rather ironic that Gaylord Perry hit the first and only home run of his baseball career six years later on July 20, 1969—just a few hours after Neil Armstrong set foot on the moon! Another version of this baseball legend attributes that statement to Perry's manager, Alvin Dark.[16] But one way or the other, it illustrates a powerful principle that is true in every sphere of life from athletics to economics. For better or for worse, our words double as self-fulfilling prophecies. Negative prophecies are validated by fear. Positive prophecies are validated by faith.

When Jim Carrey was a struggling actor trying to make it in Hollywood, he would drive up Mulholland Drive through the Santa Monica Mountains to a spot that overlooked the city of Los Angeles. Then he'd give himself a little pep talk: "Everybody wants to work with me. I'm a really good actor. I have all kinds of great movie offers." If you've seen any of his movies, it's easy to imagine him doing that, isn't it? The two-time Golden Globe winner recalled, "I'd just repeat those things over and over, literally convincing myself that I had a couple movies lined up. Then I'd drive back down, ready to take on the world." As a statement of faith, Jim Carrey wrote himself a check in the amount of $10 million, postdated it for Thanksgiving of 1995, and wrote "For services rendered" on the memo line. Then he tucked that check into his wallet to remind himself of his dream every time he opened it. By the time Thanksgiving of 1995 rolled around, Jim Carrey's asking price was $20 million per movie.[17]

I'm certainly not suggesting that you can speak whatever you want into existence with your words. Only God can do that. But if your words line up with the Word of God, miracles will happen. You will say what Jesus said and do what Jesus did. And that's precisely what Peter did. He witnessed the invalid being healed, then he followed suit not long after. On his way to the temple one day, Peter encountered a man who was lame from birth, sitting at the gate called Beautiful. Peter looked him in the eye and said, "Silver or gold I do not have, but what I do have I give to you. In the name of Jesus Christ of Nazareth, walk."[18] And just like the invalid, the lame man jumped for joy.

So let me double back to *the* question: *Do you want to get well?*

If you don't, keep doing what you're doing.

If you do, take a step of faith. Then another. And another. And if you keep putting one foot in front of the other, you'll eventually get where God wants you to go. Most miracles are the by-product of "a long obedience in the same direction."[19] You can't just take up your mat. You have to walk. And while you're walking, enjoy the journey!

12

THE RULE BREAKER

It is the Sabbath, and it is not lawful for you to take up your bed.
John 5:10 ESV

DR. EVAN O'NEILL Kane performed more than four thousand surgeries during his distinguished career as chief surgeon at Kane Summit Hospital, but his greatest contribution to medicine was as a pioneer in the use of local anesthesia. Dr. Kane believed that general anesthesia was an unnecessary risk for patients with heart conditions and allergic reactions, so he set out to prove his point by performing major surgery using nothing more than a local anesthesia. On February 15, 1921, his patient was prepped for surgery and wheeled into the operating room. After local anesthesia was administered, Dr. Kane cut the patient open, clamped the blood vessels, removed the patient's appendix, and stitched the wound. Two days after surgery, the patient was released from the hospital. The patient was none other than Dr. Evan O'Neill Kane, and his self-surgery changed standard operating room procedure.

Up until the 1968 Olympic games in Mexico City, world-class high jumpers used the straddle technique, the Western roll, or the scissors jump. Then along came Dick Fosbury. None of those traditional techniques suited his six-foot, five-and-a-half-inch body type, so Fosbury experimented with a shoulders-first, face-up technique. His high school coach opposed his unorthodox approach, but Fosbury went on to win the gold medal in Mexico and set a new Olympic record of seven feet, four-and-a-quarter inches. At the next Olympic games, twenty-eight out of forty competitors used the technique named after the man who changed his sport forever—the Fosbury Flop.

On July 29, 1588, the Spanish Armada sailed into the English Channel with the goal of turning Great Britain into a Spanish colony. Spain was the world's greatest naval power, and the Armada of 130 ships was nicknamed the Invincible Fleet. The English were outnumbered and outgunned, but they unveiled a new tactic of naval combat that changed the rules of engagement. Instead of boarding enemy ships and engaging in hand-to-hand combat, the English used long-range cannons to sink half of the Spanish fleet without losing a single ship of their own.

If you want to repeat history, do it the way it's always been done. If you want to change history, do it the way it's never been done before. History makers are rule breakers. And no one was better at it than the One who wrote the rules in the first place!

Thou Shall Offend Pharisees

Jesus could have healed the invalid on any day of the week, but He chose to perform this miracle on the Sabbath. He knew it would rile up the religious establishment, and I wonder if that's why He did it. Jesus offended the Pharisees with great intentionality and consistency. And, I might add, enjoyment.

If you follow in the footsteps of Jesus, you will offend some Pharisees along the way. In fact, there are situations where you need to go out of your way to do so. That is *not* a license to break the law. It is permission to break man-made rules that don't honor God.

Over the span of many centuries, the Pharisees compiled a comprehensive list of religious dos and don'ts called the *mitzvot*. Of the 613 codified laws, 248 were positive commands while 365 were classified as negative commands. And 39 of those prohibitions defined what was permissible and impermissible on the Sabbath—right down to the minutest detail.

Negative Mitzvah #321, for example, set the maximum walking range at 2,000 cubits. But who's counting, right? Of course, this measurement didn't start until a person was 70 ⅔ cubits outside the city limits. Practically speaking, a person could not walk in a straight line for more than .598 miles in any direction outside the city limits.[1]

While Jesus told the invalid to take up his mat and walk, He didn't tell him to hike to Timbuktu. So while the invalid probably hopped, skipped, and jumped all over Jerusalem that day, he did not go outside the parameters established by the mitzvot. Of course, it wasn't the invalid walking that caused the offense. It was the fact that he was carrying his mat—an activity that was strictly forbidden by Pharisaical law. Of course, there was *nothing* in Scripture to substantiate that regulation. And Jesus knew it since He wrote it. The prohibition against carrying a mat was not a divinely ordained law. It was nothing more than a man-made rule—and, I might add, an awfully silly rule if someone has just been healed of a thirty-eight-year-old ailment.

The great irony of this story is that while the Pharisees accused Jesus of breaking the law, they were the ones breaking the spirit of the law by trying to keep what they thought was the letter of the law. And while they thought Jesus was breaking the letter of the law, He was keeping the spirit of the law by healing the invalid.

There is a world of difference between following Jesus and following the rules. If you follow Jesus, you won't break the law of God, but you will break the rules of man. And you'll offend some Pharisees by doing so.

The Pharisees couldn't see the forest through the trees. They wanted to kill Jesus because He challenged their man-made rules. Of course, murder most definitely would have been a violation of Mosaic law! The Pharisees missed the miracle that was right in front of their eyes because they couldn't see past their human traditions and man-made rules. And that is precisely what keeps us from experiencing the miraculous as well. To experience the miraculous, sometimes you have to break the rules.

Second-Order Change

According to cybernetic theory, there are two types of change.

First-order change is behavioral—it's *doing things differently*. If you're trying to lose weight, eating less and exercising more are steps in the right direction. And first-order change can help you hit your goal. But it is incremental change that happens little by little. Second-order change is quantum change that happens all at once. It's a paradigm shift that fundamentally reframes the way we see our problems, see ourselves, or see our lives. Second-order change is conceptual— *it's seeing things differently*.

First-order change is matter over mind.

Second-order change is mind over matter.

Vision starts with visualization.

Alvaro Pascual-Leone, professor of neurology at Harvard University, validated the importance of visualization in a fascinating study involving a five-finger piano exercise. Subjects practiced the piano while neurotransmitters monitored their brain activity. As expected, neuroimaging revealed that the motor cortex was active while practicing the exercise. Then researchers told the participants to *mentally rehearse* the piano exercise in their mind. The motor cortex was just as active while mentally rehearsing as it was during physical practice. Researchers came to this conclusion: *imagined movements trigger synaptic changes at the cortical level.*[2]

That study confirmed technically what athletes already know instinctually: mental rehearsal may be just as important as physical practice. It's mind over matter.

In 1992, a Canadian swimmer named Mark Tewksbury won the gold medal in the 200-meter backstroke at the Barcelona Olympics. When he stepped onto the winner's podium, it wasn't the first time he had done so. He stood on the gold medal stand the night before the race and imagined it before it happened. He visualized every detail of the race in his mind's eye, including his come-from-behind victory by a fingertip.

In much the same way, the Australian sailing team won the 1983 America's Cup before they even set sail. Three years before the race, the coach made a tape of the Australian team beating the American team. He narrated the race himself, with the sound of a sailboat cutting through the water in the background. Every member of the team was required to listen to that tape twice a day for three years. So by the time they set sail from San Diego harbor, they had already beaten the American team 2,190 times in their mind.

Most of our problems are perceptual. The solution isn't *doing* something different. It's *thinking* about the problem differently. As Albert Einstein is said to have observed, "The significant problems we face cannot be solved at the same level of thinking we were on when we created them."[3]

According to MIT researcher Massimo Piattelli-Palmarini, most people try to solve a problem as it is presented. "Hardly ever do we spontaneously alter the formulation of a problem that is presented to us in a reasonably clear and complete way."[4] And that is precisely why many problems remain unsolved. If Jesus had tried to solve the invalid's problem as presented, He would have repositioned the man closer to the pool of Bethesda so he had pole position when the water was stirred. But that first-order change would have resulted in more of the same. So Jesus changed his life by changing the rules.

Outside the Box

The phrase "thinking outside the box" is a well-used metaphor that means to think differently. Its origins trace back to the "nine dots puzzle" employed by management consultants to teach counterintuitive problem solving. If you've performed the puzzle, you know it's easily solved. But it often seems impossible to the uninitiated.

To solve the puzzle, participants are told to connect nine dots that form a square by drawing four straight lines without lifting their pencil from the paper. The conundrum is this—if you stay within the boundaries of the box, it's impossible. And that's what most people do—they imagine a boundary around the box that isn't there. The only way to solve it is by drawing outside the lines.

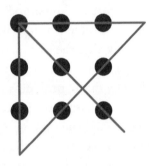

We do the very same thing with reality. Our four dimensions of space and time are like nine dots. And many of us act as if those laws are boundaries. But spiritual laws supersede physical laws. The same God who established the laws of nature can break them. The omnipresent One is not bound by space or time. He is in all places at all times. But if you want to experience the miraculous, you have to break the rules by drawing outside the lines.

Sometimes the miraculous is the difference between convergent and divergent thinking. Convergent thinking is whittling away at a problem until you find the solution to it. Divergent thinking doesn't look for one right answer. It comes up with as many solutions to the problem as possible.

Many schools and companies employ what has become known as "the brick test" to gauge a person's divergent IQ. They show a prospective student or employee an image of a brick and ask them to list all the potential uses of that brick.

People with higher convergent IQs give more conventional answers like "constructing a building with it." And there is nothing wrong with that answer! But those with higher divergent IQs give more unconventional answers like "breaking into a building by breaking a window with it." The brick test might not be a good gauge for law school, but it's probably a better predictor of Nobel Prize potential.

Divergent IQ is the ability to look at the natural and see the supernatural. It also goes by another name when anointed by the Spirit of God: faith.

Critical Realism

According to the research of Rolf Smith, children ask 125 probing questions per day. Adults, on the other hand, ask only six probing questions per day. That means that somewhere between childhood and adulthood, we lose 119 questions per day![5] At some point, most of us stop asking questions and start making assumptions. That is the day our imagination dies. It's also the day miracles stop happening. If you want to experience the miraculous, you need to quit making assumptions.

In the philosophy of science, there is a concept known as critical realism. It is the recognition that no matter how much we know, we don't know everything there is to know. In the words of Russell Stannard, "We can never expect at any stage to be absolutely certain that our scientific theories are correct and will never need further amendment."[6] What if we borrowed the concept of critical realism from science and applied it to theology? I'm not suggesting that we question any of our orthodox doctrines as revealed in God's Word. But 1 Corinthians 8:2 is a good theological starting point when it comes to the study of God: "Those who think they know something do not yet know as they ought to know."

We're too quick to explain what we don't really understand. And God is at the top of that list. You can know Him, but to think you know everything there is to know is the epitome of hubris. To know God is to enter the cloud of unknowing— the more you know, the more you know how much you don't know.

Scripture says that we can do all things through Christ who strengthens us,[7] so the words "I can't" should never leave our lips! But "I don't know" should come out of our mouths with great regularity and humility. You aren't omniscient. In fact, you aren't even close! Your best thought on your best day falls at least 15.5 billion light-years short of how good and how great God really is.

Eleven Dimensions

A hundred years ago, we thought we lived in a four-dimensional world. Then along came Albert Einstein and his theory of general relativity. He threw science a curveball by positing that the space-time continuum isn't as linear as we once thought. Then string theorists extrapolated the existence of more dimensions than meet the eye—ten dimensions in the case of superstring theory or twenty-six dimensions according to the original Bosonic string theory. In either case, this critical dimension is necessary to ensure the vanishing of the conformal anomaly of the worldsheet. And if you have no idea what that means, I've made my point. If the universe is infinitely more complex than can be imagined with the human mind, then how much more so the Creator Himself? His infinite complexity demands a degree of critical realism called humility.

If string theorists are right, then God is operating in at least eleven dimensions of space-time. And therein lies our greatest shortcoming: *putting four-dimensional limits on the Almighty*. In the words of Dr. Hugh Ross, "Orthodox Christians potentially underestimate God's nature, powers, and capacities by at least a factor of a trillion in one time dimension."[8] Multiply a trillion by a minimum of seven additional space-time dimensions, and we begin to understand why Scripture states that God is able to do *immeasurably more* than all we can ask or imagine![9] We can't even imagine one extra dimension!

Half of faith is *learning what we don't know*. The other half is *unlearning what we do know*. And the second half is far more difficult than the first half. That's why Jesus repeatedly said, "You have heard that it was said . . . but I tell you." He was uninstalling Old Testament assumptions with New Testament revelations. Going the extra mile or turning the other cheek was more than behavior modification. Jesus was reverse engineering the old rules and installing new ones.

In 1932, a German physicist named Werner Heisenberg won the Nobel Prize in Physics for his work on quantum mechanics. His discovery ranks as one of the greatest scientific revolutions in the twentieth century. For hundreds of years, determinism ruled the day. Physicists believed in a clockwork universe that was measurable and predictable. Heisenberg pulled the rug out from the under the scientific community. Here is Heisenberg's uncertainty principle in a nutshell: we cannot know the precise position and momentum of a quantum particle at the same time. Here's why. Sometimes matter behaves like a particle—it appears to be in one place at one time. Sometimes matter behaves like a wave—it appears to be in several places at the same time, almost like a wave on a pond. It is the duality of nature. So the imprecise measurement of initial conditions precludes the precise prediction of future outcomes. Simply put: there will always be an element of uncertainty.

Here's my translation: *God is predictably unpredictable.*
You never know exactly how or when or where God might
show up and show off. But you can be sure of this: He will
probably ask you to do something unprecedented, unorthodox, and unconventional. And if you have the courage to do
something you haven't done in thirty-eight years, you might
just experience something you haven't seen in a long, long
time.

THE FOURTH SIGN

Some time after this, Jesus crossed to the far shore of the Sea of Galilee (that is, the Sea of Tiberias), and a great crowd of people followed him because they saw the signs he had performed by healing the sick. Then Jesus went up on a mountainside and sat down with his disciples. The Jewish Passover Festival was near.

When Jesus looked up and saw a great crowd coming toward him, he said to Philip, "Where shall we buy bread for these people to eat?" He asked this only to test him, for he already had in mind what he was going to do.

Philip answered him, "It would take more than half a year's wages to buy enough bread for each one to have a bite!"

Another of his disciples, Andrew, Simon Peter's brother, spoke up, "Here is a boy with five small barley loaves and two small fish, but how far will they go among so many?"

Jesus said, "Have the people sit down." There was plenty of grass in that place, and they sat down (about five thousand men were there). Jesus then took the loaves, gave thanks, and distributed to those who were seated as much as they wanted. He did the same with the fish.

When they had all had enough to eat, he said to his disciples, "Gather the pieces that are left over. Let nothing be wasted." So they gathered them and filled twelve baskets with the pieces of the five barley loaves left over by those who had eaten.

John 6:1–13

13

TWO FISH

Here is a boy with five small barley loaves and two small fish, but how far will they go among so many?

John 6:9

FILET MIGNON WITH a bleu cheese crust, extra butter sauce. On special occasions Lora and I sometimes visit one of our favorite restaurants, Ruth's Chris Steak House. It's a food pilgrimage. I start eating strategically twenty-four hours in advance to maximize the meal. I also start salivating several hours prior to the reservation. When the waiter sets that sizzling steak on the table, I feel like I'm at the marriage supper of the Lamb. I worship God with every bite. By the time dessert is served, revival is about to break out.

Good food is one of God's most gracious gifts, and another one of my personal favorites is Lou Malnati's pizza. If you want to bribe me, simply send a four-pack of deep-dish pepperoni via UPS. One of the greatest moments of my life, right after watching my wife walk down the aisle on our wedding day and the births of our three children, was making my very own pizza in Lou Malnati's kitchen at the invitation of their COO. Several times a year, we ship Malnati's from Chicago because I haven't yet convinced them to open one in DC.

Now let me get very vulnerable: I'm a little possessive when it comes to Malnati's pizza. When our kids were younger, Lora and I would eat the Malnati's, but we'd put a regular store-bought pizza in the oven for our kids. That may sound cruel, but they weren't ready. They hadn't reached the age of accountability yet, and I was afraid they wouldn't be mature enough to truly steward it.

All of that to say this: if I share my Malnati's with you, *I love you. A lot.*

Hold that thought.

The focal point of the fourth miracle is Jesus feeding the five thousand with five loaves and two fish. Of course, whoever dubbed it the feeding of the five thousand shortchanged Jesus. There were five thousand *men*. So the total head count was probably closer to twenty thousand men, women, and children. Jesus doesn't just pull a rabbit out of a hat. He pulls out twenty thousand fish. But before we bite into the main entrée, we should take a look at a miracle that precedes it. An appetizer, if you will. And it's served up by a busboy of sorts.

The Pre-Miracle

Let's assume the disciples didn't strong-arm this little boy or steal his brown bag lunch. This boy gave it willingly. Then it was as much an expression of love as me sharing my Malnati's. Perhaps even more! It was also the pre-miracle that set up the miracle.

If you have young children, you have a unique appreciation for what you're about to read. Getting kids to share anything takes a minor miracle! Their favorite word is *mine*, and they say it about everything, including what's yours. Getting them to share something they *love*, like their favorite food? That takes a major miracle!

This one act of sacrificial giving was the catalyst for one of Jesus' most amazing miracles. And for the record, I don't see it as *one* miracle. It was twenty thousand separate miracles—it was a miracle for every single person there that day!

If this boy didn't share his five loaves and two fish, I don't believe this miracle of multiplication would have gone down. Am I suggesting Jesus could not have performed this miracle without the little boy's lunch? Yes and no. I suppose He could have created a four-course meal out of nothing, ex nihilo. But generally speaking, God doesn't do the supernatural if we don't pull our weight by doing the natural.

The lesson embedded in this miracle is so simple: if you put what you have in your hands into God's hands, He can make a lot out of a little!

In the natural world, it's easy to think that if you *give more*, you'll *have less*. But that's not how it works in God's economy. Things don't add up incrementally. They *multiply* exponentially! In God's economy, $5 + 2 \neq 7$. When you add God to the equation, 5 loaves + 2 fish = 5,000 meals with 12 doggie bags left over! You have more left over than you had to begin with!

Run the Numbers

The total population of the Galilee region was approximately forty thousand at the time of Christ. So roughly half of them crossed the Sea of Galilee by boat or hiked by foot to get to the mountainside where Jesus had set up camp. When Scripture says Jesus "saw a great crowd coming toward him,"[1] it's no understatement. It must have felt like Max Yasgur's dairy farm on August 15, 1969—the opening day of Woodstock.

Jesus turns to Philip and asks, "Where shall we buy bread for these people to eat?"[2]

It only makes sense that He would ask Philip because Philip was from Bethsaida, nine miles away. If anyone knew where to get food, it would be Philip. But there was no Panera Bread around the corner! And even if there was, he knew they couldn't afford to feed everyone.

His response borders on rebuke: "It would take more than half a year's wages to buy enough bread for each one to have a bite!"[3]

Translation: *Bethsaida, we have a problem!*

Over the years National Community Church has hosted a few Convoy of Hope outreaches. The largest one drew a crowd of ten thousand people, and we gave away a hundred thousand pounds of groceries. But here's the thing: we had an entire year to plan it. And it was still chaotic trying to coordinate the hundreds of volunteers it took to pull it off.

At face value this situation looks like a logistical and financial nightmare!

According to the Convention Industry Council Manual, a seated banquet requires 13.5 square feet per person. If you do the math, 13.5 square feet multiplied by 20,000 people totals 6.2 acres. The volume of food, number of waiters, and quantity of port-a-johns required to pull off this one meal is absolutely astronomical. And I'd hate to be the one stuck with dish duty!

Philip wasn't the keeper of the money bag, but it didn't take Judas to figure out that this lunch would break the bank. Just hiring the wait staff would have set them back thousands. And even if everyone ordered off the dollar menu, the meal would have cost tens of thousands.

A Drop in the Bucket

It's so easy to let what we cannot do keep us from doing what we can.

A few years ago researchers at Carnegie Mellon University devised a study to discover why people respond to the needs of others.[4] Participants were given an envelope with a charity request letter from Save the Children. The researchers tested two versions of a request letter; the first version featured statistics about the magnitude of the problems facing children in Africa, while the second letter spotlighted the needs of one seven-year-old girl named Rokia.

On average, the participants who read the statistical letter contributed $1.14.

The people who read about Rokia gave $2.38—more than twice as much.

The smaller donations in response to the statistical letter were the result of something psychologists call the "drop in the bucket effect." If we feel overwhelmed by the scale of the problem, we often don't do anything about it because we don't think we can make a difference. So statistics about massive human suffering in Africa can actually make us *less* charitable! Focusing on statistics can short-circuit a compassionate response by shifting people into an analytical frame of mind. And thinking analytically can hinder people's ability to act compassionately. The head gets in the way of the heart. The researchers came to this conclusion: the mere act of calculation reduces compassion. It reduces miracles too!

Now let's double back to the fourth miracle.

When the little boy offered to share his lunch, Andrew's reaction was, "Thanks, but no thanks!" He didn't think it would make a difference: "How far will they go among so many?"[5] But Andrew was overanalyzing the situation, and he almost missed the miracle because of it.

I have no idea how the boy with two fish scored on the math portion of the SAT, but I'm fairly certain he knew that $2 + 2 = 4$. He knew his two fish weren't enough to make a dent, let alone feed twenty thousand people! It was a drop in the bucket. But he didn't let what he *didn't have* keep him from giving what he *did have* to Jesus. And that is the precursor to many a miracle!

Like so many unsung heroes in the Bible, this little boy walks off the pages of Scripture never to be heard of again. But his fifteen minutes of fame have stretched into two thousand years! And I wouldn't be surprised if he's the one serving the fish entrée at the marriage supper of the Lamb.

Food Miracles

I love food and I love miracles, so I really love food miracles.

One of my favorites occurred while the Israelites are wandering in the wilderness.[6] Fresh manna was miraculously delivered to their front door every day, but the Israelites got tired of the same menu day in and day out. So they started complaining. Amazing, isn't it? They were literally complaining about a *miracle*!

Despite their incessant whining, God patiently responded with one of the most unfathomable promises in Scripture. Feeding two million people is no easy task, especially when you're in the middle of nowheresville. A one-course meal of meat would take a miracle. But God promised them meat to eat for an entire month. And Moses naturally had a hard time believing it. He said to God:

> Here I am among six hundred thousand men on foot and you say, "I will give you meat to eat for a whole month!" Would they have enough if flocks and herds were slaughtered for them? Would they have enough if all the fish in the sea were caught for them?[7]

Moses is doing the math in his mind, and it just doesn't add up. Not even close! He is trying to think of any conceivable way that God could fulfill this promise, and he can't think of a single scenario. He doesn't see how God can fulfill His impossible promise for a day, let alone a month.

Have you ever been there?

You know God wants you to take the job that pays less, but you won't be able to pay off your school loans. You know God wants you to go on the mission trip, but you can't afford the days off. You know God wants you to adopt a child or go to grad school or give to a kingdom cause, but it just doesn't fit in your budget.

What do you do when the will of God doesn't add up?

In my experience, the will of God rarely adds up. By definition, a God-ordained dream will always be *beyond your resources* and *beyond your ability*. In other words, you cannot afford it and you cannot accomplish it. Not in your lifetime! But God can do more in *one day* than you can accomplish in a hundred lifetimes. And He owns the cattle on a thousand hills![8]

Your job is *not* to crunch numbers and audit the will of God. After all, the will of God is not a zero sum game. When you add God to the equation, His output always exceeds your input. And your two fish can go a lot further than you imagine if you put them into His hands.

The Law of Measure

When National Community Church was getting off the ground, we had very few people and even less money. We'd start services with a dozen people, and our total income was $2000 a month. So our entire church budget wasn't much more than one person making minimum wage! I refer to them as the lean years, but I wouldn't trade those tough financial times. Living from offering to offering is living by faith. And it did more than just stretch our faith. It laid a foundation that helps us steward every penny of what is now a multi-million-dollar budget.

During our first few years, National Community Church could not afford to pay me a full-time salary. In fact, the church wasn't even self-supporting until our third year. It was the generosity of those who didn't even attend our church that kept us afloat. The financial turning point happened at the end of our first year. That's when I felt a prompting that we needed to start giving to missions. Honestly, it didn't add up at the time. In fact, it didn't even seem like good stewardship! How can you give what you do not have? Plus, we were the missionaries. We needed God to prompt others to give to us! Yet I knew that if we held on to our five loaves and two fish, we'd have five loaves and two fish. But if we dared to put some of it back in God's hands, He might be able to do something miraculous with it. So we cut our first $50 check to missions.

Last year, our congregation took twenty-five mission trips and gave $1.8 million to missions. We want to grow more so that we can give more. And we dream of the day when we deploy a mission team fifty-two weeks a year!

We operate from a simple core conviction: *God will bless us in proportion to how we give to missions and how we care for the poor in our city.* If you were the Lord of the Harvest, wouldn't you? I believe that as long as we focus on those things that are near and dear to the heart of our heavenly Father, He will take care of our bottom line. And that conviction traces back to a $50 check. When we started giving to missions, God started multiplying our two fish. The very next month, our income tripled from $2000 to $6000 a month, and we never looked back. I have only one explanation for the multiplication of our income:

> Give, and it will be given to you. A good measure, pressed down, shaken together and running over, will be poured into your lap. For with the measure you use, it will be measured to you.[9]

The law of measures is as inviolable as the law of gravity! With the measure you use, it will be measured unto you. It doesn't matter whether it's two fish or two mites, you can take it to the bank. You cannot break the law of measures, and that's good news if you're willing to give your brown bag lunch to Jesus.

Over the past three years, National Community Church has experienced multiple financial miracles. We retired a $3 million debt. We raised $3 million in three months to build a Dream Center in an underserved part of DC. And we purchased an $8 million piece of property in the heart of DC where we'll build a future campus.

It doesn't add up, but God has made it multiply.

Take It to the Bank

Moses couldn't figure out how God was going to deliver on His promissory note, but that didn't keep him from cashing it. And God paid him in the currency of quail:

> Now a wind went out from the LORD and drove quail in from the sea. It scattered them up to two cubits deep all around the camp, as far as a day's walk in any direction. All that day and night and all the next day the people went out and gathered quail. No one gathered less than ten homers.[10]

Based on the Hebrew system of measurement, a day's walk was approximately fifteen miles in any direction. So if you square the radius and multiply by pi, we're talking about an area that was about 700 square miles. That's ten times the size of Washington, DC, and the quail were piled three-feet deep!

Can you imagine seeing that many birds fly into the camp? The cloud of birds was so massive it caused a fowl eclipse. And when it started raining birds, it must have felt like Quailmageddon.

Once the quail stopped falling, the Israelites started gathering. Each Israelite gathered no less than ten homers. Assuming the quail were of average size, total accumulation was approximately one hundred five million quail. You read that right, but let me translate to numbers: 105,000,000 quail.

Sometimes God shows up. Sometimes God shows off.

One of the reasons I love this miracle is because it's a pun of biblical proportions. This miracle is recorded in the book of Numbers. The Greek name for Numbers is *arithmoi*, which is where we get our word *arithmetic*. So recorded in the book of arithmetic is a miracle that does not add up, not even close!

But with God, it's always cloudy with a chance of quail.

14

LORD ALGEBRA

He asked this only to test him, for he already had in mind
what he was going to do.

John 6:6

F EW PEOPLE HAVE witnessed more miracles than George
Müller.

Along with pastoring one church for sixty-six years, Müller
established the Ashley Down orphanage in Bristol, England.
He cared for 10,024 orphans while establishing 117 schools
for their education throughout England. Adjusted for inflation, George Müller raised $150 million dollars for those
kingdom causes. That is an incredible sum of money by any
standard, but what makes it even more remarkable is the fact
that George Müller never asked anyone for anything—not a
single penny. He made a covenant to ask *only* God. Müller
figured that God knew exactly what he needed and when he
needed it, and God could make provision for it. It is estimated
that Müller experienced thirty thousand specific answers to

prayer, as recorded in his journal. Time and time again, food was dropped off on their doorstep right when they ran out, a donation was made right before a bill came due, or a plumber offered his services right when a problem needed to be fixed.

I live by an Oswald Chambers maxim: "Let God be as original with other people as He is with you."[1] So I'm not prescribing George Müller's methodology across the board. I think it's okay to verbalize a need or ask for help, but shouldn't we put it to prayer *first* rather than last? And why do we take matters into our own hands when we can put them into the hands of God? Few things are harder than *letting go and letting God*, but that's what George Müller modeled. And I can think of thirty thousand reasons to follow his example!

Remember the Lord's Prayer? "Give us this day our daily bread."[2]

What we really wish is that it said *weekly* or *monthly* or *yearly* bread. That way we wouldn't have to depend on Him on a daily basis! But that's when God has us right where He wants us. Spiritual maturity is not self-sufficiency. In fact, our desire for self-sufficiency is a subtle expression of our sinful nature. It's a desire to get to a place where we don't need God. We want God to provide more so we need Him less. And that brings us right back to where we started: everyone wants a miracle, but no one wants to be in a situation that necessitates one. But you cannot have one without the other. So God gracefully puts us in situations where *enough isn't enough*. We find ourselves in a situation where we need to feed 20,000 people and we have two fish to our name.

The Manna Miracle

Ten years ago, National Community Church purchased an old crack house and converted it into Ebenezer's coffeehouse.

And it took a miracle just to get the contract. Not only did we purchase it for $325,000, less than one-third of the original $1 million asking price, but we also discovered that four people offered more money for it than we did. So we celebrated the miracle, but not for long, because we needed another one! We had thirty days to come up with the 10 percent down payment or the contract would be null and void. Twenty-nine days later, we had exhausted all options and we were $7,500 short.

I have a core conviction: *when God gives a vision, He makes provision*. But He often waits until the last moment. The day before our deadline, we received two checks in the mail that totaled exactly $7,500. The amazing thing is that the people who gave those gifts didn't even know the need. Both couples had moved away from the area but continued tithing to NCC until they found a new home church. I later discovered that one of those gifts was larger than normal because it was a signing bonus from a former Supreme Court clerk who had taken a job with a law firm halfway across the country.

When God miraculously provided manna for the Israelites, Scripture says that He provided just enough. The language describing God's provision is extremely precise. Those who gathered a lot "did not have too much" and those who gathered a little "did not have too little." God provided *just enough*. Then He gave them a curious command: not to keep any of it overnight.[3]

Why does God provide just enough? Why would God forbid leftovers? What's wrong with taking a little initiative and gathering enough manna for two days or two weeks?

Here's my take: the manna was a daily reminder of their daily dependence upon God.

Not much has changed. We still need a daily reminder of our dependence upon God. So while we may want a one-year supply of mercy, His mercies are new every morning. If God provided too much too soon, we'd lose our raw dependence upon God, our raw hunger for God. So God usually provides just enough, just in time.

I have scribbled the initials JEJIT in the margins of my Bible at various places where God provides just enough, just in time. He does it with the widow who is down to her last jar of olive oil.[4] He does it when the Israelites are trapped between the Egyptian army and Red Sea.[5] He does it when the boat is about to capsize on the Sea of Galilee during the perfect storm.[6]

He does it again with two fish and twenty thousand hungry people.

Ring the Bell

I'm not sure what the dinner ritual looks like at your house, but we call our kids to the dinner table when the food is almost ready to be served. If we time it right, they have just enough time to wash their hands and pour a drink. Then I pray a short prayer because I believe it's good stewardship to eat a hot meal while it's hot.

Never once have I called the kids to an empty table. Of course, now that I mention it, that might be a really good object lesson! It might help us identify with the millions who go to bed with aching stomachs every day. It might also accentuate the absurdity of the fourth miracle. Jesus says:

Have the people sit down.[7]

Jesus rings the dinner bell, but the table is empty! He has everybody take a seat, as if they're going to eat. He even blesses the imaginary meal. But as it stands, He's going to have to split two fish twenty thousand ways!

Have you ever had to wait for a meal longer than expected? Or had a waiter tell you they ran out of whatever you ordered?

The longer you have to wait, the hungrier and grumpier you get. It can get very ugly very fast. And anyone who has worked in the food service industry knows what I'm talking about. This may not seem like a dangerous situation, but if dinner isn't served, this crowd of twenty thousand turns into a mob.

That's why this prayer ranks as one of Jesus' most amazing. He is so calm and collected. John doesn't reference Jesus' prayer, but the other Gospels do, and it's the same prayer He prays at the Last Supper. In both instances I'm not sure that my words would be dripping with gratitude. But Jesus gives thanks.

Jesus thanks His Father for something He doesn't have.

Jesus thanks His Father for something that hasn't happened yet.

Lord Algebra

Up until the sixteenth century, mathematics was divided into two subfields: arithmetic and geometry. Then the French mathematician, François Viète, pioneered a new field called algebra. In doing so, he submarined the SAT scores of the mathematically challenged and probably kept you out of the college you wanted to get into.

Advanced Algebra ranks as one of my all-time least favorite classes, right before Trigonometry and right after Calculus. I didn't get it then, and I still don't get it now. But it helps me appreciate one of the hats Jesus wore: teacher. He didn't just teach religion. He also taught math. And I wonder if that is the hardest subject to teach.

Jesus was so brilliant at designing tests that half the time His disciples didn't even know they were taking them! And Philip is a good example:

[Jesus] asked this only to test him, for he already had in mind what he was going to do.[8]

The disciples had already failed Algebra I.

When Jesus fed the four thousand with seven loaves, it should have given them the faith to believe that He could feed five thousand with five loaves![9] But the lesson was lost on them. In fact, they acted as if it was their first day in class. So Jesus graciously gives them a make up test. He doesn't just teach them a new equation: $5 + 2 + X = 5,000 \, R12$. Lord Algebra gives them an object lesson.

If the first miracle reveals that nothing is too small for God. The fourth miracle counterbalances it: *nothing is too big for God*. And Jesus is the X factor.

A Factor of Thirty

I love the fact that the fourth miracle includes specific numbers. It makes the miracle more measurable, more tangible. And while we have to be careful not to make ratios out of these rations, they are not irrelevant. We count things that count. So shouldn't we count miracles the way we count offerings?

A member of our prayer team recently told me that we had thirty documented healings at National Community Church year-to-date. I was absolutely ignorant of that fact. And ignorance is like a lack of oxygen—it asphyxiates faith. That's why we need to share testimonies!

Hearing a testimony is the way I *borrow faith from others*.

Sharing my testimony is the way I *loan my faith to others*.

If we aren't sharing testimonies, we're cutting off circulation to the body of Christ. Part of the body becomes numb. And we don't just lose feeling in that part of the body. If it is starved of testimony long enough, it will eventually die. So we need to celebrate what we want to see more of.

Our testimonies of what God has done in the past become prophecies of what God will do in the future. If you start sharing testimonies of miraculous conversions to Christ, you'll see more of those miracles happen. The same is true of healing or deliverance or provision. It's like inhaling pure oxygen. It not only regenerates your faith but also charges the atmosphere of a church so that it becomes highly combustible.

When I discovered that we had thirty documented healings, it stretched my faith. I'm believing God for *more* miracles! And that's the point. It's like my faith was multiplied by a factor of thirty because there have been thirty healings. In the same way, I think the faith of the disciples was multiplied by a factor of twenty thousand.

The Multiplication Anointing

Before the release of my first book, *In a Pit with a Lion on a Snowy Day*, I was speaking at a conference in Baltimore, Maryland. After speaking, I sat in on a session with Tommy Barnett, who cofounded the LA Dream Center with his son, Matthew. Tommy shared about their providential purchase of the 360,000-square-foot Queen of Angels Hospital that sits on 8.8 acres of prime real estate overlooking Highway 101 in LA. The owners turned down lucrative offers from major Hollywood studios that wanted to turn the hospital into a movie set and sold it instead to the Dream Center for a fraction of their original asking price. The Dream Center bought it for pennies on the dollar!

The LA Dream Center now touches fifty thousand lives every month through its hundreds of ministries, and I've seen it firsthand, having spoken there several times. It has also inspired more than a hundred Dream Centers across the country, including our Dream Center in Washington, DC. In fact, Matthew spoke at NCC the weekend we cast the vision to our congregation.

After sharing his testimony, Tommy Barnett invited anyone who wanted what he called a "multiplication anointing" to come to the altar. At the time I wasn't sure if the idea of a multiplication anointing was even in the Bible. But if Tommy Barnett was laying it down, I was picking it up. I knew I needed it. And of course, this concept of multiplication is part of the kingdom math Jesus teaches via the parable of the good soil.[10]

Every author is all too familiar with this sobering statistic: 95 percent of books don't sell five thousand copies. And first-time authors sell, on average, only nine hundred copies. That's more than a little depressing, considering how hard it is to write a book. So I went to the altar and prayed for a multiplication anointing on my first book. I mustered all the faith I could and prayed that it would sell twenty-five thousand copies. That was my magic number, but the God who is able to do immeasurably more than all we can ask or imagine has exceeded my original expectations by a quarter million copies and counting.

Before you read any further, please hear my heart.

I pray that God will put my books into the right hands at the right time. And the testimonies I've heard from readers whose lives have been impacted by one sentence or one paragraph or one page from one of my books is incredibly gratifying. But I don't write for readers. I write because I'm called by God to write. Typing on a keyboard is an act of obedience, first and foremost.

That's why I don't view a book sold as a book sold.

I see it as a *prayer answered*.

I've now published ten titles, and each time a new book releases, it feels like giving God my two little fish. Once the final edits are done, it's out of my hands. I cannot control what happens, but that's the exciting part. I've had books that have been bitter disappointments while others have exceeded all expectations. All I can do is trust that God will multiply what little I have to offer and feed the multitudes with it.

When *The Circle Maker* released, a trusted friend sent me a picture of his prayer journal with the number "3.5 million" circled. That's how many copies he felt God had impressed on him to pray for. And it's well on its way. The number of times God answers that prayer is *His* business. That's way beyond my pay grade. But God does want to stretch your faith so that your biggest dreams will someday seem incredibly small. My number for my first book was a stretch eight years ago, but the multiplication anointing continues to up the ante. And I share that to share this once again: the way you steward a miracle is by believing God for even bigger and better miracles!

One Hundred Fold

One of my life goals is to give back more to National Community Church than we've received in cumulative income. Before I got my first publishing contract, that seemed like an impossible goal to achieve. How can you give more than you make? But if you keep giving God your two fish, you never know how many times He'll multiply it. Someday you may be *giving* more than you are currently *making*! It goes back to the parable of the good soil:

> Still other seed fell on good soil, where it produced a crop—a hundred, sixty or thirty times what was sown.[11]

The Old Testament tithe was more than an act of obedience—it was a statement of faith. Farmers wouldn't wait
until their entire crop was harvested and then give God the
last 10 percent. They gave God the firstfruits. In other words,
they took the first 10 percent to the temple. Then and only
then did they harvest the rest of their crop. By giving the first
10 percent, they showed that they trusted God for the other
90 percent.

If you want to experience the miraculous, sometimes you
have to give what you don't have. Don't wait until you have
two birds in your hand. Don't even wait until you have two
birds in the bush.

Lora and I grew up in a church that was focused on missions. And the way we gave to missions was something called
a faith promise. A faith promise was an amount of money
pledged to missions above and beyond the tithe. It wasn't
based on a budget. It was based on faith. And it was the
by-product of prayer. I made my first promise when I was
in high school. I can't remember how much I pledged, but
it took quite a bit of faith because I was making minimum
wage at Quick Fill gas station in Naperville, Illinois. That
faith promise was one of the first financial steps of faith I
took, and it taught me to trust God. Even then I saw Him
provide in small yet remarkable ways.

Now let me fast-forward.

In 2005 Lora and I made the largest faith promise of our
lives. We wanted to put ourselves in a position where it would
take a miracle to fulfill our promise. And that's exactly what
happened. A few months after making that faith promise, I
signed my first book contract. I don't think those two things
are unrelated. The advance on that contract made our big
faith promise seem small. And the lesson was not lost on us.
Every time I sign a new book deal, we up the ante by giving

a greater percentage back to God. And if we keep sowing the seed, we fully trust that God will continue multiplying by a factor of thirty, sixty, or one hundred fold.

It turns giving into a game.

And God always wins!

15

COUNT THE FISH

So they gathered them and filled twelve baskets with the pieces
of the five barley loaves left over by those who had eaten.

John 6:13

MY FRIEND JOEL Clark is an author and filmmaker. In
fact, we've collaborated on a fantastical trilogy for
children titled *Jack Staples*, which we prayerfully hope may
turn into a feature film someday. Along with having off-the-
charts creative gifts, Joel is also one of the most compassionate people I know. Much of his film work has focused on
documenting the pain and suffering of those who don't live
in the land of opportunity. But Joel wasn't always that way.

For nearly a decade, Joel served on staff at a church in South
Africa. During that time his relationship with God became
more professional than personal. He was low on money and
even lower on morale. His heart was hardening and so was
his hearing. But that dramatically changed during a late-night

McDonald's run. The 38 rand in his pocket was just enough to indulge himself in a Happy Meal. Joel was so focused on his own issues that he barely noticed the street kids in the McDonald's parking lot. Then, for the first time in a long time, Joel heard that still small voice of the Holy Spirit: *Buy those kids some hamburgers!*

Joel had a decision to make: order a Happy Meal for himself or buy burgers for those street kids. He didn't have enough money to do both. "I was filled with bitterness and pettiness," Joel said. "Even though I ordered five junior cheeseburgers for those kids, I didn't do it with the right attitude." But despite Joel's doing the right thing with the wrong attitude, God still showed up and showed off.

When Joel walked out the door of McDonald's, the group of streets kids had doubled. Joel contemplated cutting the burgers in half so everyone could have one. But when he started handing them out, they multiplied like the Filet-O-Fish that fed five thousand. Did McDonald's give him the wrong order? Did they throw in extras because it was closing time? Or did God reach into His bag of tricks and simply pull out some junior cheeseburgers? Joel has no idea to this day, but when he had given a burger to every street kid, he found one extra at the bottom of the bag for himself.

Joel calls it his McMoment. And the lesson was not lost on him: if you give your Happy Meal to Jesus, it'll go a lot further in His hands than it would in your stomach. It'll taste better too!

If you keep giving, God will keep multiplying.

The Giving Game

When Lora and I got married, we made a decision that we would never *not* tithe. Giving God the first 10 percent of our income isn't a decision we make every time we get a paycheck. It's a pre-decision we made on day one, and it's been paying dividends ever since! That pre-decision was a pre-miracle. But tithing isn't the end goal. It's just a starting point. Our ultimate goal is to reverse tithe—to live off of 10 percent and give 90 percent back to God. And the way we've tried to get there is by giving God a greater percentage of our income every year. I call it "The Giving Game." And the irony of this game is that you cannot win. And you cannot win for one simple reason: you cannot out-give God. But it sure is fun losing the game to God.

For the record, I don't believe in the prosperity gospel.

When you add something to the gospel, you actually subtract from it. The gospel, in its purest form, is as good as it gets. The gospel is *not* a get-rich-quick scheme! In fact, the goal is to end up dirt poor by giving away as much as you can. Am I suggesting that you shouldn't plan for retirement or invest in a 401(k) or leave an inheritance to your kids? I'm most certainly not. But saving for retirement isn't the goal of the game. If you think that God wants to pad your pockets so you can live in a bigger house or drive a nicer car, you have bought into a false gospel. It's not about raising your standard of living. It's about raising your standard of *giving*. When God blesses you more, it's so that you can be more of a blessing. A tangible earthly reward for giving is the least return on investment. The goal of the Giving Game is storing up treasures in heaven. That's the eternal dividend.

Trust me when I say that God cannot and will not be bribed or blackmailed. You cannot play Him like a slot machine. If you give simply because you want to get something in return, you forfeit your down payment. You can't play the game that way. We invest in the kingdom of God because it's the right thing to do and it nets the best return on investment. Nothing beats compound interest for eternity! But if you give for the wrong reasons, you're disqualified.

Now let me flip the coin.

God will never shortchange you.

A selfish mindset believes that the more you give, the less you'll have. It thinks in terms of addition and subtraction. A miraculous mindset believes the exact opposite: the more you give, the more God can provide. It thinks in terms of multiplication.

Lora and I have certainly had our fair share of tough financial times, but those tough times have taught us to appreciate everything we have as a gift from God. Contentment isn't getting what you want. It's appreciating what you have! And the more you give, the more you enjoy what you keep! If you give God the tithe, you'll enjoy the 90 percent you keep 10 percent more. And if you double tithe, it'll double your enjoyment.

We've also learned that one of the surest ways to experience a miracle yourself is to be part of someone else's miracle. Isn't that what the little boy did? He got to have his cake and eat it too! When you try to be a blessing to others, God has a way of making the blessing boomerang.

A $15,000 Miracle

Several years ago, we did a sermon series titled "Miracles" at National Community Church. After one of those messages, I felt led to invite anyone who needed a miracle to come forward for prayer. At one of our locations, a woman named Renee Reed responded. Renee leads a mission organization called Global Outreach, and she told me they needed $15,000 to complete construction on an orphanage in Uvira, Congo. As I prayed for Renee, I felt like the Holy Spirit stirred my spirit: *Why are you praying for something when you can do something about it?* So after praying, we took a special offering. One week later, we gave Renee a $15,000 check. And like many of the miracles I've experienced, it has reproduced itself and multiplied in unpredictable ways.

The following year, a team from NCC went to the Congo to work with that orphanage, and we've returned every year since. Our projects have ranged from planting onions to teaching English to establishing a medical clinic to running a Vacation Bible School for the fifty-seven orphans who live at the Congo for Christ Center (CCC).

Our office manager, Sarah Bayot, has co-led that team every year. She's also organized her team to compete in a "Tough Mudder" obstacle race to raise funds for CCC. And this year, she felt led to quit her job at NCC and devote her full time and talent to the mission in Congo by creating an organization called Kicheko.[1] Sarah shared her vision for producing goods that benefit CCC at an annual event called A18 Innovate where ordinary NCC members share the extraordinary ways in which they are fulfilling the Great Commission. During her talk, someone in the audience felt led by God to give her entire life savings to Sarah's kingdom cause. Lindsay isn't a wealthy executive or professional investor. She's a senior in college! But she didn't let that keep her from writing a $15,000 check to Kicheko. And the blessing continues to boomerang!

One footnote: I love the way Lindsay discovered National Community Church. She was at a white elephant exchange where she received a copy of *In a Pit with a Lion on a Snowy Day*. After reading it, she started attending. Now that's a supernatural synchronicity. And she's now a shareholder in the ongoing miracle of what God is doing through the Congo for Christ Center.

Standard of Giving

Few people have played the Giving Game better than John Wesley. He was a better giver than he was a preacher, which is saying something. He lived by a simple maxim: "Make all you can. Save all you can. Give all you can." During his lifetime, Wesley gave away approximately 30,000 pounds. Adjusted for inflation, that equals $1,764,705.88 in today's dollars.

The genesis of Wesley's generosity was a covenant he made with God in 1731. He decided to limit his expenses so he had more margin to give. His income ceiling was 28 pounds. That first year, John Wesley only made 30 pounds, so he gave just 2 pounds. The next year, however, his income doubled. And because he continued living on 28 pounds, he had 32 pounds to give away. By the third year, his income increased to 90 pounds. And because he kept his expenses flat, he was able to double down on his giving.

Wesley's goal was to give away all excess income after bills were paid and family needs were taken care of. He never had more than 100 pounds in his possession because he was afraid of storing up earthly treasure. Even when his income rose into the thousands of pounds, he didn't interpret God's blessing as permission to live large. John Wesley died with a few coins in his pocket, but he had a bankroll in heaven.

Don't be discouraged by how little you may have to give. It may seem like a drop in the bucket, but it can make as much of a difference as the little boy's two fish. And the point of the Giving Game isn't how much you give, it's how much you keep. The one who has the least left at the end of their life wins! The most celebrated giver in the Gospels is the widow who gave next to nothing.[2] She won the Giving Game with two mites! But she won because she kept *nothing* for herself.

Beyond Your Ability

God cannot give back what you don't give away. It's as simple as that. And that's why many of us never experience His miraculous multiplication. Here's one secret to experiencing the miraculous: if you give beyond your ability, God will multiply it beyond your ability.

Nearly every financial breakthrough I've witnessed, both personally and corporately as a church, traces back to a financial step of faith. Before National Community Church could afford to pay me a full-time salary, I felt compelled to sow a seed into another ministry in DC. I felt like the Lord was testing us, just like He tested Philip. So we wrote a $350 check. I don't remember how we arrived at that number, but it was way beyond our budget at the time. In fact, we had to watch our bank balance so it didn't bounce.

I'll never forget putting that check in an envelope and dropping it in the mailbox outside the Post Office at 45 L Street SW. It wasn't easy to let go of it! Then I walked inside to check my PO Box. That's when I found an envelope with a return address I didn't recognize. Inside that trifold letter was a check for $10,000.

That's a 2,757.1 percent return on investment in sixty seconds flat. And for a split second, I think I felt the same adrenaline surge the disciples must have felt when Jesus turned two fish into twenty thousand. I'll be the first to admit that the Giving Game doesn't always work this way or this quickly. Again, most of our reward is not tangible. It's in a safety deposit box that we can't access until we enter eternity. But sometimes God connects the dots between the cause and effect, the natural and supernatural, faith and the miracle. This was one of those moments. And after you experience a miracle like this, it's hard not to give with a measure of holy anticipation.

Generosity is one of our four family values. And in case you care, the other three are gratitude, humility, and courage. In my experience, gratitude and generosity are next of kin. If your heart is filled with gratitude, it's easy to give! And generosity positions us to experience the miraculous. It's no coincidence that the miracle of multiplication takes place right after Jesus says *thanks*. It's not a magical word, but it is a biblical word. And when you *give thanks* and *give money*, God will multiply your gifts exponentially.

Seven and a Half Feet

This book revolves around the seven miracles in John's Gospel, but I have a confession to make. There is an eighth miracle, the miraculous catch of fish, tucked away in the back of John's book.[3] It's a bonus miracle, a miracle-to-go.

I don't know the first thing about fishing. That is a sad reality given the fact that I was born in Minnesota, the land of ten thousand lakes. Our family vacationed on one of them, Lake Ida, every year until I turned twenty-one. And every year we had a friendly little fishing contest, which I never won. My brother Don is the fish whisperer in our family. The fish would feast on his lures. My lures, sometimes the same exact daredevil as his, would usually net a famine.

So I know next to nothing about fishing, but there is one thing I know for sure: fishermen count fish. They measure their weight. They measure their length. And they most definitely tally their total catch. That's why the specificity of the eighth miracle doesn't surprise me at all. I'm guessing they actually counted two or three times to cross-check the exact number. I'm not sure what an average fishing trip would net, but they had been fishing all night with no luck whatsoever. The fish simply weren't biting. Then Jesus told them to fish on the other side of the boat. And that's where we need to zoom out.

First-century fishing boats were seven and a half feet wide. So what's the point of trying the other side?

What difference does ninety inches make?

Then Jesus gives them an unforgettable object lesson: sometimes ninety inches is the distance between 0 and 153. You may be only seven and a half feet from a miracle—but you have to try the other side!

Miracles don't just happen when we believe God for big things. Miracles happen when we obey God in the little things. When we do little things like they are big things, God will do big things like they are little things.

What I love about the miracles involving fish is that it's the one sphere where the disciples might have been tempted to assert superiority. I'm sure they would have never verbalized it, but I wonder if they honestly believed that they knew a thing or two about fishing that Jesus didn't. After all, Jesus was a carpenter. They were practically born in a fishing boat. This was their domain. This was their strong suit. And that is often where it is hardest to trust God. We start trusting in our God-given gifts instead of the God who gave them to us in the first place.

Lord Ichthyoid

Throughout history, some of the church's most brilliant scholars have speculated on the significance of the number 153. Jerome referenced Oppian's *Halieutica*, which cited 153 species of fish in the Sea of Galilee. Augustine of Hippo noted that 153 is the sum of the first 17 integers, making it a triangular number. He also claimed that 17 is the perfect combination of law and grace: the Ten Commandments plus 7 gifts of the Spirit.

Evagrius Ponticus further expounded on the mathematical properties of 153 by noting that 100 is a square number, 28 is a triangular number, and 25 is a circular number.

To be candid, I don't think the number 153 was included for the sake of symbolism. If in fact there are 153 species of fish in the Sea of Galilee and the disciples caught one of each kind, that would certainly increase style points. But I don't think that's the point. I think the specificity challenges us to measure our miracles. "Count the fish" is shorthand for "measure the miracle."

Yes, miracles are mysterious. But our faith wasn't meant to be nebulous. Not every miracle can be quantified, but the ones that can be, must be. Isn't that why Jesus sent the lepers to see the priest? He wanted the miracle to be validated. If magnetic resonance imaging had been available, the before and after pictures of some of Jesus' miracles would have been worth more than a thousand words. We need to measure our miracles with X-rays, with dollars, with facts, with numbers, with tests, with pictures. We need to count miracles the way we count blessings. The latter amplifies joy while the former fortifies faith.

When Jesus told the disciples to try the other side of the boat, they could have taken offense. "Don't tell us how to do our job. We know this lake better than you do. We're the ones who've been fishing all night." And if they had taken offense, they would have missed the miracle.

What do you do when God's logic doesn't line up with yours? When the will of God doesn't add up? When you think you know better or know more than God?

Try following the example Peter set the first time Jesus multiplied a catch of fish:

Master, we've worked hard all night and haven't caught anything. But because you say so, I will let down the nets.[4]

Peter took Him at His word: *"Because you say so."*

Sometimes faith is as simple as the old adage: God said it. I believe it. That settles it. Of course, you might have to take a ninety-inch step of faith as well.

Are you willing to try the other side of the boat?

THE FIFTH SIGN

When evening came, his disciples went down to the lake, where they got into a boat and set off across the lake for Capernaum. By now it was dark, and Jesus had not yet joined them. A strong wind was blowing and the waters grew rough. When they had rowed about three or four miles, they saw Jesus approaching the boat, walking on the water; and they were frightened. But he said to them, "It is I; don't be afraid." Then they were willing to take him into the boat, and immediately the boat reached the shore where they were heading.

John 6:16–21

16

THE WATER WALKER

When they had rowed three or four miles, they saw Jesus
walking on the sea.

John 6:19 ESV

A METEOROLOGICAL MIRACLE MAY be the reason why the
capital of the United States is located in Washington,
DC. I first heard this little-known legend from a Congressman
during a late-night tour of the Capitol building, but firsthand
witnesses and secondhand evidence substantiate his story.

On August 24, 1814, a four-thousand-member British force
led by General Robert Ross marched into Washington, DC.
Most of the eight thousand residents had already evacuated
the city, including First Lady Dolly Madison, who managed
to salvage the Declaration of Independence and Gilbert Stu-
art's full-length portrait of President George Washington.

The British began the systematic burning of the Treasury
Building, the Capitol, and the President's Palace, which was

renamed the White House after it was whitewashed to cover up smoke damage from the fire. One of the few buildings left standing was the Marine Barracks at 8th and I, kitty-corner to our Capitol Hill church campus.

Tradition has it that the British left the barracks unburned in deference to the Marine Corps. Truth be told, they probably just needed a place to bunk that night. One of the few surviving buildings, a four-story brick brownstone between the Marine Barracks and the Navy Yard, is now owned by National Community Church. It is arguably the oldest commercial building on Capitol Hill, predating the invasion of Washington by nearly a decade.

With much of the city in ashes, there was strong sentiment to move the capital from Washington back to Philadelphia where the First Continental Congress met, but the bill to relocate the capital was voted down by Congress. The swing vote was a miracle that our Founding Fathers attributed to the providence of God.

According to the *Old Farmer's Almanac*, temperatures on August 24, 1814, soared above 100 degrees Fahrenheit. As the British set fire to government buildings, there was no reprieve in sight. Then, like a company of firefighters responding to a five-alarm fire, a furious thunderstorm arrived on the scene unexpected and unannounced. Like a divine sprinkler system, the heavy rains kept the White House from completely burning to the ground.

The severe windstorm that followed spooked the British as it blew over cannons and caused barrels of gunpowder to spontaneously combust. And while weather alone may not be the reason British troops withdrew, many Redcoats believed it was a sign from God. And many members of Congress who voted to keep the capital in Washington concurred. They believed it was a sign from God, not unlike the seven miracles in John's Gospel.

Seventy-Minute Miracle

I once took a class in meteorology at the University of Chicago, and thus began my love affair with the weather. One of my favorite things to do on vacation is to watch the weather channel, which my family has great fun with. I find storm systems both entertaining and humbling.

Two thousand years ago, predicting the weather was a crapshoot. A few well-worn aphorisms were everyone's best guess: "Red sky at night, sailor's delight. Red sky in morning, sailor take warning." Of course, even with the aid of weather satellites, our best forecasts still feel like a fifty-fifty coin flip at times. We may understand Mother Nature better now than we ever have, but she is still as powerful and unpredictable as ever.

We use reinforced concrete to protect ourselves against earthquakes and storm shutters to safeguard against hurricanes, but we still cannot control the weather. All we can do is talk about it when there is nothing else to talk about. But there is One who commands the wind and rebukes the waves. The One who turned water into wine also turned the Sea of Galilee into a sea of glass. The One who created the heavens and the earth with four words can quell any squall with just three words: "Peace, be still."[1]

The Sea of Galilee is the setting for many of Jesus' miracles. Some of them happen below the surface of the water, like the miraculous catch of fish. Others happen above the surface, like stopping a tropical storm in its tracks. But the most astonishing may be the fifth miracle in John's Gospel, when Jesus turned whitecaps into a red carpet. And this was no hop, skip, or jump. The Water Walker covered at least three and a half miles! At an average walking pace of three miles per hour, this miracle most likely lasted at least seventy minutes.

The density of water is one gram per cubic centimeter at 4 degrees Celsius, which means, quite simply, that humans sink in water. The surface tension of water can support the superhydrophobic water strider, also known as the pond skater. Then there's the infamous Jesus Christ lizard, star of a must-watch YouTube video. But when it comes to the human species, we're not well equipped for water walking. If you could sprint 67 mph you could actually run on water, but the fastest recorded foot speed is 27.79 mph by Jamaican Olympic gold medalist Usain Bolt. Reaching 67 mph would require fifteen times more energy than the human body is capable of expending.[2]

Surfing the Sea of Galilee

In April 2006, *The Journal of Paleolimnology* published a paper with a rather dubious title: "Is There a Paleolimnological Explanation for 'Walking on Water' in the Sea of Galilee?" An expert in oceanography and limnology, Dr. Doron Nof, and his coauthors assert that an odd combination of atmospheric conditions may cause rare patches of floating ice on the Sea of Galilee. According to their calculations, the chances of this floating ice phenomenon happening are less than once every thousand years. But those odds didn't deter them from questioning whether Jesus walked on water after all. Perhaps Jesus just surfed a patch of floating ice.[3]

To be honest, I'm not sure which one would be more amazing. Surfing a piece of floating ice across the Sea of Galilee would take miraculous balance. And if those patches of ice appear only once every thousand years, it would take miraculous timing too. I'd love to see a high-definition, slow motion instant replay of either one—walking on water or surfing on ice. But in my humble opinion, this hypothesis reveals more about the human psyche than the circumstances surrounding Jesus' fifth miracle. We have a natural tendency to explain away what we cannot explain. And that's why most of us miss the miracle. Remember the old aphorism, "You have to see it to believe it"? It's true, but the opposite is even truer: *you have to believe it to see it.*

If you don't have a cognitive category for the supernatural, you don't know what to do with phenomena that do not compute within the logical constraints of the left brain. Like a small calculator that cannot multiply large-digit numbers, miracles register as an intellectual error. That's why the disciples didn't recognize Jesus at first. They thought He was a ghost. And our initial reaction, like theirs, is often to rebuke the revelation out of ignorance. We fear it because we don't have a memory to go with it.

Nine Dolphins

One of my favorite TED lectures is delivered by Al Seckel, an authority on visual perception and sensory illusion.[4] During the lecture, he shows the audience a stenciled drawing that they readily recognize as a couple intimately embracing. But when that same image is shown to children, almost like a Rorschach test, the children cannot see the couple. Seckel explains that the children can't see it simply because they don't have a prior memory to associate with the picture. In other words, they have no cognitive category for what they were seeing. For what it's worth, most children say they see nine dolphins.

The reason many of us miss the miracles that are all around us all the time is because we don't have a prior memory to associate with them. That's precisely why the disciples thought Jesus was a ghost. They had no cognitive category for someone walking on water.

Imagination is a function of memory. Imaginations are extrapolations of what we have seen or heard or experienced. Ideas don't materialize out of thin air, unless of course it's a God idea that bypasses the five senses and is directly revealed by the Holy Spirit. But by and large the boundary line around imagination is drawn by past experience. New experiences and new ideas expand our borders.

In his book *Mozart's Brain and the Fighter Pilot*, Richard Restak shares a profound truism: learn more, see more. He notes, "The richer my knowledge of flora and fauna of the woods, the more I'll be able to see. Our perceptions take on richness and depth as a result of all the things that we learn. What the eye sees is determined by what the brain has learned."[5]

When astronomers look into the night sky, they have a greater appreciation than others for the constellations and stars and planets. They see more because they know more. When musicians listen to a symphony, they have a greater appreciation for the chords and melodies and instrumentation. They hear more because they know more. When sommeliers sample a wine, they have a greater appreciation for the flavor, texture, and origin. They taste more because they know more.

I believe that every *ology* is a branch of theology. And this will make even more sense when we get to the man born blind. Without a basic understanding of neurology, the sixth miracle is misinterpreted and underappreciated. While we tend to think of spiritual and intellectual pursuits as mutually exclusive endeavors, that's a false dichotomy. Great love is born of great knowledge. And the more you know, the more you know how much you don't know. True knowledge doesn't puff up with pride. It humbles us until we hit our knees in worship.

It also beckons us out of the boat.

Embrace the Mystery

How do you react to the unprecedented—something for which you have no prior memory to associate it with? What do you do when God does something that defies your experience of reality? What's your response when Jesus shows up in the least likely way at the least likely time in the least likely place?

One option is to ignore the miraculous, covering your eyes like a little child playing peekaboo. Another option is disbelief. You can excise the miracles altogether, a la Thomas Jefferson. A popular postmodern option is to intellectualize the miraculous, but our attempts to outsmart the Omniscient One with sophisticated suppositions usually make us sound awfully silly. My advice? Don't try to explain it. And don't try to explain it away. Simply embrace the mystery of the miraculous! The miracles of God make us appreciate the mystery of God. They also help us see God for who He is—the Wine Maker, the Water Walker, the Grave Robber.

God is more than a subject to be studied.

He is the *object* of all wonder, all worship.

I'm not suggesting we shouldn't study to show ourselves approved, as 2 Timothy 2:15 implores us. Quite the contrary! But *systematic theology* is the ultimate oxymoron. God defies definition. He can be known, but never fully known. Again, the more you know, the more you know how much you don't know. The net result of seeking God is not just knowledge. It's mystery. And anything less than mystery is idolatry. Why? Because it's nothing more than a psychological projection—it's a human attempt to create God in our image. But what you end up with is a dumbed-down version of the gospel that is man-centered.

When it comes to syncing reality and theology, we often sync the wrong way. Doubt is downgrading your theology to match your experience of reality. Faith is the exact opposite. Instead of allowing circumstances to get between you and God, faith is putting God between you and your circumstances. It's not denying reality. It's recognizing that there is a reality that is more real than what you can perceive with your five senses. Faith is a sixth sense that enables us to perceive the impossible. And faith ultimately upgrades our reality until it syncs with theology.

One of my all-time favorite quotes is a Mark Nepo classic: "Birds don't need ornithologists to fly."[6] And water walkers don't need limnologists to walk on water! If you follow in the footsteps of Jesus long enough, you will eventually walk on water. You'll go impossible places and do unimaginable things. Water walking will become a way of life.

Boldly Go

If you grew up watching the original *Star Trek* TV series, the opening narration at the beginning of every episode is unforgettable:

> Space: the final frontier. These are the voyages of the star-ship *Enterprise*. Its five-year mission: to explore strange new worlds, to seek out new life and new civilizations, to boldly go where no man has gone before.[7]

I quote that last line, "to boldly go where no man has gone before," quite frequently. And for some reason, I think of it every time I read this verse:

> The wind blows where it wishes, and you hear its sound, but you do not know where it comes from or where it goes. So it is with everyone born of the Spirit.[8]

Translation: God is awfully good at getting us where God wants us to go, but there will be some crazy twists and turns along the way!

My friend Jeff Ellis recently shared one of those hairpin turns.

After visiting his daughter in DC, Jeff got stuck in Beltway traffic on the way to the airport and missed his flight. He was still irritated when he boarded the next available flight. Jeff found his seat and wanted nothing more than to mind his own business. That's when a very extroverted old man and his wife sat next to him. Jeff, who isn't chatty to begin with, knew it was going to be a very long flight.

Jeff happened to have a copy of *The Circle Maker*, and his seatmates noticed it. Come to find out, the man and his wife had just attended the National Prayer Breakfast. And they had missed their flight as well.

Then Jeff asked him the courtesy question, "What do you do?" During the ensuing conversation, the retired doctor told him that he was a friend of the CEO of Tyson Foods, Donnie Smith. Then his wife mentioned that their daughter had adopted two girls from Ethiopia. When Jeff asked where, they told him it was a small village named Mekelle.

Jeff may as well have been shot with a *Star Trek* stun gun. Jeff's son, David, moved to Mekelle, Ethiopia, a few years ago to start Mekelle Farms and Chicken Hatchery! In Jeff's words, "What are the odds of two people on the whole plane even knowing where Mekelle Farms is in Ethiopia, much less sitting together on a flight neither of them were scheduled to be on? And to think that the conversation started over a copy of *The Circle Maker*."

If your vision is to establish the poultry industry in Ethiopia, a meeting with the CEO of Tyson Foods doesn't hurt, does it? The doctor made a phone call, and David had the opportunity to spend a couple hours with Donnie Smith soon thereafter in Rwanda. David's chicken farm now partners with one of Tyson's subsidiaries, hatching 150,000 chicks a month and counting.

Maybe you feel like you're on the wrong plane. Let me remind you of how good God is at getting us where He wants us to go, even when it's our fault for missing a flight. You may be one seat assignment or one phone call from a miracle!

17

DARE THE DEVIL

A strong wind was blowing and the waters grew rough.

John 6:18

THEIR SURNAME IS synonymous with high-risk high-wire spectacles. Seven generations of Wallendas have performed jaw-dropping feats of balance for kings and queens and millions of circus-going kids. The most famous Flying Wallenda, Karl, died at the age of seventy-three after falling from a high wire between high-rise hotels in Puerto Rico.

Karl's great-grandson, Nik Wallenda, is the latest and perhaps greatest aerialist ever. His curriculum vitae includes seven Guinness World Records. Nik secured his place in the history books with the first tightrope crossing of Niagara Falls. The most meaningful stunt may be his re-creation of the Puerto Rico walk that claimed his great-grandfather's life. But his magnum opus is undoubtedly the unprecedented and unparalleled Grand Canyon crossing of June 22, 2013, which I watched live. He crossed the canyon on a two-inch tightrope fifteen hundred feet above the canyon floor with no safety net.

It was Nik's grandfather who impressed upon him at an early age that safety nets give a false sense of security. Therein lies one of the secrets to experiencing the miraculous: *if you want to walk on water, you've got to get out of the boat.*

I know it's been said a thousand times in a thousand ways. But like each of the secrets I've shared, it's easier said than done. Many of us fail to achieve our dreams or experience the miraculous because we're more focused on not falling than on taking the first step. Instead of going for broke, we keep filling our piggy bank or building our résumé. But there comes a moment when you need to quit preparing for the life you want to live and start living it.

When Lora and I felt God calling us to the nation's capital, we packed all of our earthly belongings into a U-Haul and moved to Washington, DC. We had no safety net—no family, no place to live, and no guaranteed salary. But we took a 595-mile step of faith because we believed that our destiny was DC. It felt like we were crossing a canyon, but we never looked down, never looked back.

More than thirteen million viewers from 217 countries watched the canyon crossing on television, breaking the Discovery Channel's ratings record. They also heard Nik pray and praise Jesus for what seemed like the longest 22 minutes and 54 seconds in television history. If everybody in the viewing audience had been hooked up to a blood-pressure machine, I'm pretty sure that high-wire act would have registered a record spike.

But when you've been walking on wires since the age of two, risk becomes second nature. For Nik Wallenda, wire walking is a way of life. He doesn't evade danger; he seeks it.

Tell him something cannot be done, and that is exactly what he will attempt to do. He's fearless, even when he's fifteen hundred feet above the Grand Canyon with thirty-mile-per-hour wind gusts.

To call Nik Wallenda a daredevil seems like an obvious understatement. After all, he stands on the shoulders of a family who does human pyramids on high wires. But Nik doesn't get that daring streak just from his DNA. I think the wire walker gets it from the Water Walker Himself.

Shock and Awe

The word *daredevil* can have negative connotations, but let me try to redeem it by redefining it. It's more than the frivolous risking of life and limb or recklessness for no good reason. Etymologically, it means *to dare the devil*. And as such, it should be a defining characteristic of anyone who follows the One who went forty rounds with the devil in the desert. Fearlessness is one of the most overlooked and underappreciated dimensions of His kaleidoscopic personality.

Jesus is the definition of *daredevil*.

I'd love to have seen the look in His eyes right before turning the tables on the money changers and stampeding their herds out of the temple with a homemade whip.[1] The most amazing part of this incident is not what Jesus did but what the temple guard did not do. Why didn't this ancient SWAT team arrest him? Shock and awe! What kind of daredevil would pull a stunt like that?

Only *the* Daredevil.

In the timeless words of Dorothy Sayers:

The people who crucified Jesus never, to do them justice, accused him of being a bore—on the contrary, they thought

him too dynamic to be safe. It has been left for later generations to muffle up that shattering personality and surround
him with an atmosphere of tedium. We have very efficiently
pared the claws of the Lion of Judah, certified him "meek
and mild," and recommended him as a fitting household pet
for pale curates and pious old ladies.[2]

If Sayers's generation declawed the Lion of Judah, we have
neutered Him. Or lobotomized His wild side. And then we
wonder why we're bored with our faith? We have given people
just enough Jesus to be bored, but not enough to transfix and
transform. The Lamb of God bleats for us, but the Lion of
Judah still roars.

The fearlessness of Jesus is epitomized by a supernatural
showdown with a demoniac named Legion.[3] Legion's nick-
name is a not-so-subtle reference to a Roman military division
that consisted of as many as six thousand soldiers. It's no
wonder this demon-possessed man could not be bound by
chains—he had the strength of six thousand demons. And
a man with a death wish is particularly dangerous. Legion
lived among the tombs—a lost cause with a lost mind.

When Jesus docked at Gerasenes, Legion saw Him from a
distance and started running toward Him. Now this is where
you have to hit the Pause button. The Bible doesn't reveal
the reaction of the disciples, but I bet they were on their
heels ready to hightail it out of there. Jesus didn't flinch. He
was absolutely fearless in the face of evil. And that's where
miracles are found—on the far side of fear.

The odds on this cage fight were 6000:1, but that didn't
keep Jesus from daring the devil. And in boxing terms, it was
a technical knockout—the demoniac fell to his knees before
the opening bell. Then Jesus dunked the devil by casting
that legion of demons into a herd of pigs that drowned in
the Sea of Galilee.

Fearlessness

In his first epistle, the apostle John outlines the objective of love:

Perfect love casts out fear.[4]

Love is more than feel-good emotions or sappy sentiments. Biblically speaking, it's synonymous with fearlessness. Love doesn't just make you weak in the knees. It makes you stand firm in your faith no matter what the circumstances—even when you come face-to-face with a legion of demons.

If you fear God, you have nothing else to fear. And that includes the devil himself. He has no license to violate your free will. He has no foothold that you do not give him via doubt or disobedience. The blood of Jesus is your shield, and the Word of God is your sword. And you can do far more than resist the devil. You can dare the devil by asserting your authority as a child of the King.

While there are several thousand classified fears and phobias, we are born with only two innate fears: the fear of falling and the fear of loud noises. Every other fear is learned, which means that every other fear can be unlearned. But the key to unlearning is a revelation of God's love. That's how your fears fade away—the fear of failure, the fear of people's opinions, the fear of the future. If you keep growing in God's love, all that will be left is the fear of God.

One of my prayers for my children is that they'll have soft hearts and strong spines. I want their hearts to be sensitized to the still small voice of the Holy Spirit. And I pray that their hearts would break for the things that break the heart of God. But I also want them to stand straight and stand strong for what's right. We live in a culture where it's wrong to say something is wrong. Not only is that wrong, but it makes it even tougher to do what's right. That's why moral courage is the rarest kind of courage. It takes a daredevil to do what's right.

The will of God is not an insurance plan.

It's a daring plan.

We are not commissioned to hold the fort until Jesus returns.

He commands us to invade enemy territory and reclaim it for righteousness.

Jesus didn't suffer a brutal death on the cross just to keep us safe and sound.

Jesus died to make us dangerous.

He died to make us daredevils.

Miracle by Moonlight

Because we're two thousand years removed from the miracles of Jesus, we often miss the minor details that make them so miraculous. We tend to overlook intangibles in the text, but the Bible is explicit:

A strong wind was blowing and the waters grew rough.[5]

Because of its low elevation, the Sea of Galilee has warmer air temperatures over it than surrounding areas. So it's not uncommon for sudden storms to sweep down the Jordan River valley. A March 1992 storm recorded ten-foot waves that significantly damaged the modern city of Tiberias. The storm system described in John's Gospel may have produced waves that were half as high or twice as high, but one way or the other, it was high tide.

Don't just read that. Let it register.

Have you ever experienced the crippling power of a wave?

I've been body-slammed while boogie boarding in the Atlantic a time or two. Even a five-foot wave can knock the wind out of you or knock you unconscious. I've done an ocean triathlon with seven-foot waves. Fighting the waves to reach the first buoy was far more difficult than crossing the finish line. And I've spent twenty hours on the high seas island-hopping in the Galápagos. Our dinghy wasn't big enough for our mission team or for the billowing waves that caused all of us to lose our lunch.

I have a friend who works with a surfing school for aspiring professionals in South Africa. He recently told me about his first time big wave surfing in Cape Town. And by big wave, I mean twenty-foot swells. To pull it off, he needed a towboard and compression jacket. The jacket wouldn't keep him from drowning, but the former world champion surfer who gave it to him told him it would keep his intestines from exploding if he took a spill.

My point?

Jesus didn't just walk on water.

He waltzed waves.

I don't know about you, but when I'm faced with a new challenge, I usually try to stack as many factors in my favor as possible. I want a warranty against failure and a guarantee of success. So in this situation, I would have waited until the wind and waves died down. And I definitely would have waited for sunrise. Not only because it would have been much safer and easier that way but because then everybody would see me do it.

Not Jesus.

Jesus does this miracle by moonlight because He wasn't seeking the limelight. It was the fourth watch of the night— right before dawn when it's darkest. That low visibility definitely increased the degree of difficulty, and I don't think the Daredevil would have had it any other way. Walking on water is impossible under any circumstances, but doing it in the middle of the night in rough waters is a little harder, a little scarier.

It's an easily overlooked detail, but why were the disciples rowing across the Sea of Galilee in the middle of the night in the middle of a storm in the first place? They were following their Captain's orders, orders I probably would have second-guessed. They had crossed the same sea earlier that day, hiked up a mountainside, and waited on a dinner party of twenty thousand. Then Jesus asks them to work the night shift by rowing back across the Sea of Galilee. The disciples were at the end of their rope, the end of themselves, but that's when you're getting close to the miracle.

Uncharted Waters

A block from Ebenezer's coffeehouse is a statue honoring one of our city's namesakes, Christopher Columbus. The inscription says: "To the memory of Christopher Columbus, whose high faith and indomitable courage gave to mankind a new world." Columbus and his crew would have never discovered the new world if they had not left the old world behind. The most amazing fact may be that prior to their history-changing voyage, not one of his crew members had ever been more than three hundred miles offshore.

In the words of Nobel Laureate André Gide, "One doesn't discover new lands without consenting to lose sight of the shore for a very long time."[6]

The Sea of Galilee is seven and a half miles wide and seventeen miles long, with a maximum depth of one hundred fifty-seven feet. John's Gospel specifically mentions that the disciples had rowed thirty furlongs, a little more than three and a half miles out to sea.[7] The significance of that is this: they were nowhere near shore. And that's where most miracles happen. They don't happen in the shallow end of the pool. They happen when you jump off the high dive into the deep end where you can't touch bottom.

That's what my friend Jack did when he moved to South Africa to disciple surfers. All he had was a few dollars in his wallet and the change in his pocket—no safety net. He thought he was going to work with a ministry called Surf Life, but God had very different plans for Jack. And that's what happens when you follow Jesus. You think you're going someplace to do something, but God often has an alternative itinerary you know nothing about. Lora and I didn't move to Washington, DC, to pastor National Community Church. It didn't even exist yet. We thought we were moving to DC to start a parachurch ministry, but God had a hidden agenda. He always does. He tells us to set sail for Capernaum, and we naturally think that is the objective. But you never know when or how or where Jesus might show up.

When Jack was twenty-six, he heard God's voice while smoking a joint on I-26 just outside Charleston, South Carolina. Now that's an unlikely circumstance. And I strongly discourage replicating those circumstances! But it does reveal God's ability to show up anywhere, anytime, anyhow. God told Jack that if he'd follow Him, He would use Jack's life to tell His story, and make a movie out of it. When Jack set sail for South Africa several years later, that promise was all but forgotten. Then Jesus entered stage right—walking on water.

Jack was hosting a large surfing outreach in Jeffreys Bay. That same day, a South African movie director named Bruce MacDonald and his production assistant were scouting out possible sets for a scene from their upcoming movie, *The*

Perfect Wave. While he was driving, Bruce sensed a still small voice prompting him to turn down one of the side streets. Bruce had surfed almost every beach in Jeffreys Bay, but he'd never seen the beach at the end of this particular block.

When he pulled into the parking lot, Bruce got out of the car, walked straight up to Jack, and asked him who he was. Something clicked in both of their spirits. Bruce had declined ten different Hollywood-caliber actors who had auditioned for the costarring role opposite Clint Eastwood's son, Scott. In what must rank as one of the strangest auditions ever, Jack did a reading for the casting director on the spot, right in the parking lot, and got the role of the wild child. Honestly, Jack didn't have to do much acting because that's who Jack was. And just like the story line of his own life, the climax of the movie is redemption.

Most miracles don't happen within sight of the shoreline. You have to row about thirty furlongs out to sea. You have to venture into uncharted waters. And if you do, don't be shocked if God surprises you by showing up in the most unlikely places at the most unlikely times. You might even mistake God for a ghost, but that is the nature of God. The Water Walker loves waltzing into our lives at crazy times and places. That's how He shows up and shows off His power.

18

Cut the Cable

It is I; don't be afraid.

John 6:20

Y OU HAVE UNDOUBTEDLY been on an elevator that bears his name. Otis elevators have been the industry standard for more than 150 years. It's estimated that the equivalent of the world's population travels on an Otis elevator, escalator, or moving walkway every three days.[1]

While Elisha Otis did not invent the elevator, the doll-maker-turned-inventor did devise the braking system that ensured its safety. It was this invention that made modern skyscrapers possible. Without a trustworthy braking system, elevators were earthbound and building heights were limited to a pedestrian six stories. With it, the sky was the limit.

Otis elevators are the primary means of vertical transportation in some of the world's tallest and most famous buildings, including the Eiffel Tower, the Sears Tower, and the Empire

State Building. Before the collapse of the Twin Towers on September 11, 2001, Otis express elevators had the capacity to carry a 10,000-pound payload 110 stories in less than one minute. Tragically, the elevator shafts turned into 1,368-foot chimneys that channeled jet fuel and funneled smoke after the first hijacked aircraft hit the North Tower at 8:46 a.m. Providentially, Otis elevators in the South Tower were the means of salvation for the thousands who would not have had time to escape by stair before Flight 175 crashed into the South Tower at 9:03 a.m.

Elisha Otis couldn't seem to sell his elevators until he concocted one of the most persuasive sales pitches in history at the Crystal Palace Exhibition in 1854. Standing atop a platform governed by his newly installed braking system, Otis ordered an axman to cut the cable. It was a stunt of Cirque du Soleil scope. Not only did the braking system halt his free fall—it skyrocketed sales.

I have some entrepreneurial friends who are cut from the same cloth as Elisha Otis. They started a company that manufactures a brand of body armor weighing less than one pound per square foot. When it comes to body armor, there is no margin for error. So to demonstrate its effectiveness, they sell their product by shooting a willing volunteer who is wearing it. They got the idea from the original designer, who had an employee shoot him with a handgun while he was wearing the armor he created.

> Faith is pulling the trigger and believing that your body armor will stop the bullet.
> Faith is cutting the cable and believing that the braking system will stop your fall.
> Faith is getting out of a boat and believing the water will hold your weight.

I don't remember who said it or where I heard it, but it's always been one of my favorite definitions of faith: *faith is climbing out on a limb, cutting it off, and watching the tree fall.* For Lora and me, it was our cross-country move to Washington, DC. We didn't just climb out on the limb. We cut it off.

In Matthew's account of this miracle, Peter walks on water as well.[2] I don't know what thoughts fired across his synapses as he stepped off the stern of that fishing boat, but he must have felt the same mixed emotion of fear-faith that Elisha Otis felt when he cut the cable. He looked like a pirate walking the plank, without the plank. But that's faith. The logical mind can see only two options when stepping out of a boat in the middle of the lake: sink or swim. That's why most people stay within the comfortable confines of the boat. That's also why most people never walk on water.

The Eye of Providence

Three Gospel writers record the miracle of Jesus walking on water. John focuses on the main act—the Water Walker Himself. The Gospel of Matthew provides the prologue and second act. The first detail Mark adds to his Spirit-inspired docudrama is the fact that Jesus sees the disciples straining at the oars.[3] We read right past that, but how did He see them? It's not like Jesus had night vision goggles or binoculars.

Technically speaking, the farthest object visible with the naked eye is the Andromeda galaxy, located 2.6 million light-years from Earth. That galaxy's one trillion stars emit enough light for a few thousand photons to hit each square centimeter of Earth every second. On a dark night, that's enough to electrify our retinas. Of course, Jesus wasn't looking up into the sky. He was looking out to sea. And the earth curves out of sight at a distance of 3.1 miles, so with the disciples three and a half miles out, they were out of visual range. Even if you account for extra distance to the horizon by virtue of the fact that Jesus had climbed a mountain when the disciples set sail, you still can't account for the fact that it would have been pitch-black. I've sailed on the Sea of Galilee after dark, and without artificial illumination, you can hardly see your hand in front of your face. Yet Jesus sees frustration on their faces from seven thousand paces. That is a miracle within a miracle.

It reveals once again that God is great not just because nothing is too big for Him. God is great because nothing is too small. He cares about every minute detail of your life! If it's a big deal to you, it's a big deal to Him.

There are more than four hundred names for God in Scripture, each one revealing a different dimension of His kaleidoscopic personality. He is Jehovah Jireh—the God who provides. He is Jehovah Rapha—the God who heals. And one of my personal favorites, He is Jehovah Roi—the God who sees.

Our founding fathers called it the Eye of Providence. They so esteemed His providential care that they commissioned the Swiss artist Pierre Eugene du Simitiere to incorporate the all-seeing eye into his design of the Great Seal of the United States. Every time you pull out a one-dollar bill, His eye is on you. And His eye is on the sparrow. And His eye was on His friends who were fighting high waves and headwinds on the Sea of Galilee.

This isn't the first farsighted miracle in John's Gospel. Remember Jesus' encounter with Nathanael? Jesus said, "I saw you while you were still under the fig tree."[4] It's a mysterious allusion to what must have been a defining moment in Nathanael's life. And Nathanael experiences a quantum leap of faith. He goes from, "Nazareth! Can anything good come from there?" to "Rabbi, you are the Son of God" in a split second.⁵ All because Jesus could see around corners!

The Invisible Hand

Our first president, George Washington, may have had a more profound appreciation for the Eye of Providence than anyone of his generation. On April 30, 1789, he delivered his first inaugural address, paying homage to God's providence in his life and the life of his country. He said:

> No people can be bound to acknowledge and adore the Invisible Hand which conducts the affairs of men more than those of the United States. Every step by which they have advanced to the character of an independent nation seems to have been distinguished by some token of providential agency.⁶

Those were not words spoken in a vacuum. They had poignant personal meaning. As President Washington stood on the balcony of the Federal Hall in New York City, he must have experienced a forty-four-year flashback to the Battle of Monongahela in July of 1755. The then twenty-three-year-old colonel in the British army had two horses shot out from under him and four musket balls pass through his coat. A Native American named Redhawk later testified to having shot at Washington no less than eleven times. He was convinced that Washington was bulletproof. Of the thirteen hundred British soldiers, only thirty survived. And every other officer on a horse besides George Washington was killed. In a letter to his brother, Washington wrote, "Death was leveling my companions on every side of me, but by the all-powerful dispensations of Providence, I have been protected."⁷

Fifteen years after that battle, Washington returned to the wilderness territory in the Western Reserve where he encountered the same tribe of Native Americans. Not surprisingly, the chief recognized Washington immediately. The average soldier fighting in the Revolutionary War was five foot one. Washington was no less than six foot two. Their dialogue was first recorded in George Bancroft's *History of the United States*, published in 1838.

Through an interpreter, the tribal chief made a startling prophecy of biblical proportions:

> I am the chief and ruler over my tribes. My influence extends to the waters of the great lakes and to the far blue mountains. I have traveled a long and weary path, that I might see the young warrior of the great battle [Washington].
>
> It was on the day when the white man's blood mixed with the streams of our forest, that I first beheld this chief [Washington]. I called to my young men and said, "Mark yon tall and daring warrior? He is not of the redcoat tribe—he hath an Indian's wisdom, and his warriors fight as we do—himself alone is exposed. Quick let your aim be certain, and he dies." Our rifles were leveled, rifles which but for him, knew not how to miss. Twas all in vain; a power mightier far than we shielded him from harm. He cannot die in battle.
>
> I am old, and soon shall be gathered to the great council fire of my fathers in the land of shades, but ere I go, there is something that bids me speak in the voice of prophecy: Listen! The Great Spirit protects that man, and guides his destinies—he will become the chief of nations, and a people yet unborn will hail him as the founder of a mighty empire.[8]

Those prophetic words were spoken long before the Declaration of Independence was signed or the shot heard round the world triggered the Revolutionary War. Before America became America, our unique destiny as a nation was prophesied by a Native American who recognized the providence of God when he saw it.[9]

To the All-Seeing Eye, there is no past, present, or future. There is no here or there. The Omniscient One sees all and knows all. He has infinite insight and eternal foresight. One thing God is not capable of saying is, "I didn't see that coming." Nothing catches Him by surprise. In fact, He made provision for every contingency in human history before the creation of the universe.

Miracles are simply peepholes into His providential care. They are the intersections where power and compassion parade God's glory. The fifth miracle is not some stunt by a sidewalk magician. It's more than a display of mind-boggling buoyancy. It's a picture of Jesus compassionately responding to His friends whose strength was spent.

Beaten by the Waves

The fifth miracle is uniquely personal for me because of a traumatic experience from my childhood. While on vacation at Lake Ida in Alexandria, Minnesota, I got up early one morning to get a jump on our family fishing contest.

It was the first time I'd ever taken the nine-foot aluminum rowboat out by myself, and I snuck out of the cabin without anybody knowing because I didn't want to wake up my brother. It wasn't until I was two hundred yards offshore that I realized a strong tailwind was blowing me out into the lake. I tried rowing back, but it was a losing battle. That's when fear gripped my ten-year-old heart. For a split second, I thought about jumping out of the boat and swimming to shore, but it would have been the worst and possibly last decision of my life. Instead, I stood up and started frantically waving my hands and yelling, hoping that someone would see or hear me.

Fortunately, a couple of old anglers who were eating breakfast came to my rescue. By the time they got to me, I had drifted to the other side of the lake. They helped me into their boat and started towing my rowboat back to Bedman's Beach.

In the meantime, my parents formed a search party when they discovered that their son and rowboat were missing. They got into a speedboat to crisscross the lake looking for me. That's when they saw a couple of fishermen towing an empty rowboat. Their hearts skipped a beat because they couldn't see me huddled under a towel behind the bow of their boat. I've never seen my parents madder or gladder—they didn't know whether to hug me or spank me. And I'll never forget the sinking feeling of being thoroughly beaten by the wind and waves. It was acute fear coupled with a feeling of futility.

The crew aboard the SS *Apostle* were seaworthy fishermen, not ten-year-old amateur anglers. But Matthew chooses his words carefully: "beaten by the waves."[10] The disciples were fighting a losing battle.

Listen, if you're fighting cancer or fighting for your marriage, there are days when you feel beaten by waves of discouragement. Or maybe you're drowning in a sea of debt. I know it's a sinking feeling, but you cannot have a comeback without a setback. Remember what was said at the outset? Everyone wants a miracle, but no one wants to be in a situation that necessitates one! We want smooth sailing, but that's sailing away from the miraculous. The prerequisite is often a perfect storm. And it's that moment when you feel helpless and hopeless when God's omnipotence overwhelms your impotence like a fifty-foot tsunami.

Act Two

I have a confession to make: I scream during scary movies. I try to muffle the screams, but you don't want to be anywhere near my elbows if we're watching anything with aliens in it.

My dad took me to see Steven Spielberg's *Close Encounters of the Third Kind* when I was seven and I'm still getting over it. Your popcorn and ICEE drink are not safe if you're sitting next to me.

My reaction to scary movie scenes is probably a pretty good approximation of how the disciples reacted when they saw Jesus walking on the water. Matthew says they "cried out in fear."[11] And he should know because he was there! *Shriek* might be a better translation. The disciples screamed like little girls. And I don't think Jesus let them forget it. He probably reenacted it a time or two when He wanted to get a good laugh. Can't you see Jesus hiding behind corners and jumping out to elicit the same scream?

The initial reaction of the disciples is sheer terror. In fact, they thought they saw a ghost. But it's Peter's "take two" that Matthew spotlights:

> Lord, if it is you, command me to come to you on the water.[12]

Peter gets a bum rap as the disciple who denied Jesus, but he's the only one who got close enough to get caught. He's also the only disciple who dared to go overboard. Matthew reveals that Peter lost focus and lost faith. He took his eyes off of Jesus and sank into the sea, but at least he got out of the boat. And for a split second, he walked on water!

In my experience, those who criticize water walkers typically do so from the comfortable confines of the boat. The more you accomplish for the kingdom of God, the less critical you become. Failure makes us more forgiving. Water walkers would rather make mistakes than miss opportunities. They'd rather sink than sit.

But let me give you one rule of thumb. If you're going to get out of a boat in the middle of the Sea of Galilee in the middle of the night, you better make sure Jesus said, "Come."

Of course, if Jesus says, "Come," you better not stay in the boat. Is it easy to discern the difference? No. But I'd rather stub my toe than sit on my backside. After all, you can't be the hands and feet of Jesus as long as you're sitting on your butt.

Make no mistake, inaction is an action. And those inaction regrets will haunt us the rest of our lives. We'll die wondering *what if?* But if you get out of the boat, you might just walk on water.

There comes a moment when you need to take a radical step of faith. And that moment will define every moment that follows. The first step is always the longest and the hardest. But to borrow the sentiments of a moon walker named Neil Armstrong, that one small step can turn into a giant leap.

THE SIXTH SIGN

As he went along, he saw a man blind from birth. His disciples asked him, "Rabbi, who sinned, this man or his parents, that he was born blind?"

"Neither this man nor his parents sinned," said Jesus, "but this happened so that the works of God might be displayed in him. As long as it is day, we must do the works of him who sent me. Night is coming, when no one can work. While I am in the world, I am the light of the world."

After saying this, he spit on the ground, made some mud with the saliva, and put it on the man's eyes. "Go," he told him, "wash in the Pool of Siloam" (this word means "Sent"). So the man went and washed, and came home seeing.

His neighbors and those who had formerly seen him begging asked, "Isn't this the same man who used to sit and beg?" Some claimed that he was.

Others said, "No, he only looks like him."

But he himself insisted, "I am the man."

"How then were your eyes opened?" they asked.

He replied, "The man they call Jesus made some mud and put it on my eyes. He told me to go to Siloam and wash. So I went and washed, and then I could see."

John 9:1–11

19

NEVER SAY NEVER

Nobody has ever heard of opening the eyes of a man born blind.

John 9:32

IN THE MIDDLE of the South Pacific, a tiny island called Pingelap dots the map. Its total landmass is less than three square miles and the highest elevation on the island is just ten feet above sea level. So when Typhoon Lengkieki swept over the island in 1755, it destroyed all of its vegetation and drowned 90 percent of its inhabitants. The twenty survivors resorted to fishing as the only means of survival until the island revegetated.

After the great typhoon, a genetic peculiarity evolved. A surprisingly large proportion of the next generation was born color-blind. Elsewhere in the world, less than one in thirty thousand people are color-blind. On the island of Pingelap, one in twelve is born with the condition. The high percentage can be traced to the fact that several people in the surviving gene pool carried a rare genetic mutation responsible for congenital achromatopsia.

Those of us with normal color vision have approximately seven million cones in our eyes that enable us to distinguish ten million different colors. Achromatopes have no functional cones. They rely exclusively on their low-light photoreceptor rods in the retina. As a result, they are so hypersensitive to light that they wear very dark wraparound sunglasses or avoid light altogether. And their poor visual acuity forces them to use a monocle to read text or see things from a distance.

The sad irony is that few places on earth are as beautiful or colorful as this tropical paradise. "It was striking how green everything was in Pingelap," notes Oliver Sacks in his book *The Island of the Colorblind*. "Not only the foliage of trees, but their fruits as well."[1] The brightly colored exotic fruits look as good as they taste, but the color-blind Pingelapians cannot perceive those Crayola colors because of one genetic mutation.

Geneticists have discovered four causes of congenital achromatopsia. Three of them are mutations in the cone cell cyclic nucleotide-gated ion channels CNGA3 and CNGB3, as well as the cone cell transducin, GNAT2. The most recent discovery is a mutation of gene PDE6C, located on chromosome locus 10, 10q24.

When was the last time you thanked God for chromosome locus 10, 10q24? Or for any of those cells or chromosomes?

The Mind's Eye

At about six months of age, children start developing internal pictures of external realities. Psychologists refer to this ability to create and catalog mental images as representational intelligence. Like a slow-developing Polaroid, those internal images are developed in the darkroom of your mind's eye.

The first internal image is mom, which develops at about six months of age. Dad doesn't enter the picture until about eight months. Give children a few years, and their entire vocabulary will have a matching picture. But if your eyesight doesn't develop normally, neither will your mind's eye.

To the seeing eye, words prompt images.

If I say *the White House,* a picture of 1600 Pennsylvania Avenue pops into your mind. And the same is true of *lake* or *car* or *pet.* We all fill in the blanks differently, but we have images to match those words. I see Lake Ida in Alexandria, Minnesota; my first car, a 1985 Dodge Colt affectionately referred to as the Batmobile; and our dog, Mickey.

What does that have to do with the sixth sign?

The man born blind had as many words in his vocabulary as we do, but zero images. His photo album was empty—a pictureless existence. He couldn't picture the faces of his mother or father. He'd heard his friends describe the beauty of the lily and the splendor of the Jerusalem sunset, but he couldn't imagine them because he had never seen them. He'd never even seen himself in the mirror, so he literally had no self-image. He couldn't even pick himself out of a lineup.

Imagine closing your eyes and never being able to open them again. Your world would go dark, but in the darkroom of your mind you can still develop pictures of images you've seen before. But if your eyes had never been opened to begin with, your mind would draw blanks. This was the only world the man born blind had ever known.

It's hard to imagine this miraculous moment because we cannot unsee what we've seen, but I think we'll experience something similar when we cross the space-time continuum. Our glorified bodies will include glorified senses. We'll hear angelic octaves that were inaudible with earthly ears and see celestial colors that were invisible with earthly eyes.

What will we see first?

Ironically, I think we'll see exactly what the man born blind saw first—the face of Jesus.

Good Eye

During my senior year of high school, my basketball coach noticed I was squinting at the free throw line, so he suggested I get my vision checked out. I honestly thought my vision was normal, but the ophthalmologist informed me that I had 20/40 vision. I was seeing at twenty feet what people with normal vision could see at forty feet, which might explain my shooting percentage from the free throw line.

You can function pretty effectively with 20/40 vision—you can get your driver's license, read print, and recognize faces. But you lack acuity. And distant objects look blurry.

I will never forget the car ride home after putting in contacts for the first time. I almost can't put it into words. It was only a five-minute drive, and we'd made that drive a thousand times. But it was like I was seeing the world for the very first time! I remember seeing some pink and purple flowers that were so vivid and so colorful and so beautiful I could hardly believe my eyes.

I was finally able to see what had always been there.

The man born blind had to be overwhelmed by the images flying at him, but he saw them for what they are—miracles.

> Your eye is the lamp of your body. When your eye is healthy, your whole body is full of light, but when it is bad, your body is full of darkness.[2]

We don't see the world as it is. We see the world as we are.

I can't read this verse without hearing my Little League baseball coach yelling, "Good eye, good eye!" In the baseball context, it means not swinging at bad pitches. In the biblical context, it means looking at things from a God's-eye view. And when you look at life through your good eye, you discover that there is more to everything than meets the eye!

The only difference between seeing the miracles and not seeing them is which eye we're looking with. Jewish rabbis made a distinction between a *good eye* and *bad eye*. Both had to do with a person's attitude toward others. A bad eye turned a blind eye to the poor. A good eye referred to a person's ability to see and seize every opportunity to be a blessing toward others.

Every *Ology*

I split my undergrad education between polar opposites— the University of Chicago and Central Bible College. But I wouldn't trade either one. The curriculum at Central laid a theological foundation as I studied everything from pneumatology to soteriology to eschatology.[3] But if you asked me which undergraduate class had the greatest influence on my theology, I would have to say it was a class on immunology at the University of Chicago Hospital Center. The irony is that my professor didn't refer to God once in her lectures. I'm not even sure she believed in God. But every lecture on the immune system was a brilliant exegesis of Psalm 139:14: "I praise you because I am fearfully and wonderfully made." I remember walking out of one of those classes praising God for hemoglobin!

That class not only gave me a profound appreciation for the intricacies of the immune system; it also conceived in me a deeply held conviction that *every ology is a branch of theology.*

While Scripture belongs in a category by itself as special revelation, God has revealed different facets of who He is through nature. And if you turn a blind eye to natural revelation, special revelation isn't as special. Albert Einstein said it best: "Science without religion is lame, and conversely, religion without science is blind."[4]

Whether they know it or not, the astronomer who charts the stars, the geneticist who maps the genome, the oceanographer who explores the barrier reef, the ornithologist who studies and preserves rare bird species, the physicist who tries to catch quarks, and the chemist who synthesizes chemical compounds into pharmaceutical drugs are all indirectly studying the Creator by studying His creation.

There will always be scientists who reject the existence of the One who created their curriculum, but just because they keep faith out of the equation of science doesn't mean we should keep science out of the equation of faith. In my experience, science adds dimensionality to theology. That's why my library is filled with books on a wide variety of subjects ranging from entomology to neurology to ophthalmology. And while I may know just enough about those subjects to be dangerous, they have infinitely increased my appreciation for the Creator and His creation.

Science is a poor substitute for Scripture but makes a wonderful complement to it. In fact, some miracles don't make sense without it. And the sixth miracle is one of them. Just as a little chemistry enhances our appreciation of Jesus mutating water molecules, a little neurology goes a long way toward explaining the miraculous healing of a man born blind.

Synaptogenesis

Most of us take our eyesight for granted unless we lose it, but even the simplest process is divinely complex. The retina, for example, conducts close to ten billion calculations every second, and that's before an image even travels through the optic nerve to the visual cortex. Dr. John Stevens puts it this way:

> To simulate 10 milliseconds of the complete processing of even a single nerve cell from the retina would require about 500 simultaneous non-linear differential equations one hundred times and would take at least several minutes of processing on a Cray supercomputer. Keeping in mind that there are more than 10 million cells interacting with each other in complex ways, it would take a minimum of a hundred years of Cray time to simulate what takes place in your eye every second.[5]

Honestly, I have no idea what that even means. And that is precisely my point.

> Ears that hear and eyes that see—the LORD has made them both.[6]

Verses like this one go in one ear and out the other. We don't even do a double take, but it would take a lifetime of research to exegete and appreciate all the optical and auditory nuances of just this one verse of Scripture. But the sixth miracle goes way beyond healing blind eyes.

Four primary types of healing miracles are repeated in the Gospels. Jesus made the lame walk, the mute talk, the blind see, and the deaf hear. While all four are amazing in their own right, blindness certainly entails the greatest degree of difficulty because of the complexity of the human eye. But the sixth miracle is in a category all by itself. Jesus doesn't just heal a blind man; He heals a man *born* blind. The significance of that is this: there were no synaptic connections between the optic nerve and visual cortex in this blind man's brain.

This healing miracle wasn't as simple as correcting an astigmatism, healing a corneal scar, or removing a cataract.

Jesus hardwires this blind man's brain by creating a synaptic pathway that did not exist.

This is nothing short of synaptogenesis.

On day forty-two after conception, the first neuron is formed in a baby's brain. By birth a baby will have an estimated eighty-six billion brain cells.[7] As a newborn experiences new sights and sounds, the brain begins to form neuronal connections called synapses. Almost like telephone wires that crisscross a city, synapses crisscross the cerebral cortex. By the time a baby is just six months old, each brain cell has about eighteen thousand connections. Maybe more if you choose the right developmental music and videos like Baby Mozart CDs or Baby Einstein DVDs. But no pressure!

This miraculous process is called synaptogenesis, and in my humble opinion, synaptogenesis is almost as amazing as Genesis itself. If the human mind is God's magnum opus, then synaptogenesis is Symphony No. 5 in C Minor.

Dr. Harry Chugani, the pediatric neurologist who pioneered PET scans, compares the process to a nuclear reactor. Millions of neurons are firing across billions of neural pathways every second of every day. According to Dr. Chugani, a baby's brain pulsates at about 225 times the rate of the average adult. If you're a parent, that just about explains everything, doesn't it? No wonder it's so hard to keep them constrained in a high chair!

Never Say Never

Did you know that babies are born legally blind?

I must have missed that memo! But maybe it's a blessing in disguise. The faces we make at newborn babies might scare them and scar them if they could see them.

At birth, their vision is no better than 20/200, and they cannot focus on anything farther than twelve inches away. That's why touch is so critical in the early stages of a baby's life. That's how they interpret the world. After eight months, however, their visual acuity, color vision, and depth perception rival that of the adult making silly faces at them.

During this developmental process, windows of opportunity open and close like clockwork. Vision, for example, is primarily wired between birth and eighteen months, and synaptogenesis in the visual cortex peaks at about three months. That's where this miracle gets fascinating. If you were to place a patch over the eye of a newborn baby and leave it there during the first few years of life, that baby would be blind in that eye for the rest of their life, even if there was no physical deformity or genetic defect. The reason is simple: no synapses would form between the visual cortex and optical nerve.

Now double back to the man born blind.

Ophthalmologists would call his condition irreversible. The natural window of opportunity had closed. But that's when God performs some of His greatest miracles. The child-bearing years had passed Sarah by many moons before Isaac was born, but that didn't keep God from opening a supernatural window of opportunity and delivering on His promise. And that postmenopausal miracle is bookended by the virgin birth. Before the natural window of opportunity opened for Mary, the Son of God was conceived by the Spirit of God.

Do you ever feel like you've missed your window of opportunity?

Maybe you've lost count of how many specialists you've gone to or how many treatments you've taken. Your last marriage ended in divorce and you're not sure if you can love someone, let alone trust someone, again. Or repeated mistakes seem to have sabotaged whatever integrity you had. Or a social stigma has ostracized you from friends and family. Or you feel so sexually broken that you aren't even sure what healthy sexuality looks like or feels like anymore.

Those aren't hypotheticals. Those are the people Jesus healed—the woman with the issue of blood, the woman at the well, the tax collector, the leper, and the woman caught in the act of adultery.

I don't know your specific circumstances, but I do know that God can create a new synaptic pathway or repair an old one. He is the God of second chances, and third and fourth and thousandth.

It's never too little.

It's never too late.

When Jesus gets involved, *never say never*!

20

THE MIRACLE LEAGUE

Who sinned, this man or his parents, that he was born blind?

John 9:2

MY FRIENDS JOHN and Tricia Tiller experienced a parent's worst nightmare when their three-year-old son accidentally fell out of a second-story playroom window. Eli was medivaced to the hospital where he was comatose for three weeks. He miraculously survived, but not without significant brain damage. Eli had to relearn every basic motor function from speech to mobility. And despite the prayers of his parents and endless hours of physical therapy, Eli still has significant limitations. He has limited peripheral vision out of both eyes, and the left side of his body has limited motor skills. So Eli speaks with a severe stutter and walks with a pronounced limp, but he has the voice of an angel and the sweet spirit to match. His pitch isn't perfect, but there wasn't a dry eye when he sang "I Will Rise" at National Community Church.

John and Tricia have thanked God countless times for saving their son, but their prayers for miraculous healing have gone unanswered. They've done everything humanly possible to help their son and spent tens of thousands of dollars on uninsured medical equipment. For the first three years postsurgery, they spent 80 percent of every waking hour in therapy. And they continued to believe that God was going to heal their son. In John's words, "We waited and waited. We knew that one day we'd be standing in front of crowds saying, 'Look what the Lord has done! He has completely healed our son.' But that's not what happened."

What do you do when the miracle you're believing God for doesn't happen? When no matter how hard you pray or how long you wait, your day never comes?

Sometimes you need to keep holding out for the miracle, like the woman with the issue of blood who held out and held on for twelve long years.[1] But sometimes you need to accept the new normal and recognize that God might want to glorify Himself in a way you wouldn't choose. And it takes tremendous spiritual discernment to know when to believe what. In John's words:

> After three years of doing everything we could for our son, it was time to accept his current condition and choose to live life with disability. This disability was something we couldn't remove, and evidently God was choosing to not completely heal Eli. So we had to burn our old scripts and look for what God could do with our new script. So for the past five years, we've accepted life with disability. That doesn't mean I've stopped praying for my son. Like any father, I'd give my right arm to see my son healed. But instead of getting discouraged or getting angry, I choose to look for what God can do.[2]

Why, God?

In the aftermath of the accident, when life went back to normal for everyone not immediately affected by it, John dueled with doubt. He began to interrogate God with *why* questions:

> "Why, God? Why do little boys fall from windows? Why did my little boy fall from that window? Why him? Why me?" I looked to Scripture for an answer, and it turns out that "Why, God?" is not a new question at all.[3]

John found the answer to his question in John's Gospel. The family and friends of the man born blind made a false assumption—an assumption that added insult to injury, an assumption that inflicted undue emotional pain and suffering. It was hard enough being blind, but to carry the weight of responsibility for something that wasn't his fault must have been nearly unbearable. The false assumption is evidenced by the question they ask Jesus: "Who sinned, this man or his parents?"[4] They assumed it was a generational curse, a sin issue, or a lack of faith. But it was none of the above. Then Jesus set the record straight by revealing the real reason:

> This happened so that the works of God might be displayed in him.[5]

When life doesn't go according to plan, we naturally look for someone or something to blame. That tendency goes all the way back to the Garden of Eden when Eve coined the excuse, "The devil made me do it." But no one wins at the blame game! And it's usually followed by a postgame pity party.

At some point, we must recognize that the circumstances we ask God to change are often the very circumstances God is using to change us. We don't always get an answer to our *why* questions on this side of eternity, but sometimes God leaves clues.

Like any normal father, John dreamed of playing catch in the backyard with his son. That's something Eli isn't able to do. Eli will never make it to the Big Leagues, but he was drafted by the Miracle League—a baseball league for kids with special needs. At first, John was afraid that he was setting up his son to fail. But there is only one rule in the Miracle League—every kid gets a hit, every kid gets on base, and every kid scores! They play on a rubberized field for wheelchair accessibility, and each kid has a teenage or adult buddy.

"If you saw them play," John says, "you'd call it a miracle."

Sometimes the miracle we want isn't the one we get. God gives us a different one. It might not be our first choice, but it's not second best.

About a year ago, the Miracle League did a black-tie fundraiser hosted by the local minor league baseball team. A few major leaguers, including pitching sensation Javier Lopez, showed up. But it was Eli who stole the show by leading the crowd in a rousing rendition of "Take Me Out to the Ball Game." Once again, there wasn't a dry eye in the ballroom! Eli has that effect. By the end of the night, Eli helped them raise lots of money so other kids like him could play ball too. He even signed a few autographs!

There are lots of chapters yet to be written in Eli's life, but John can now see the story line God is authoring in and through his son. He says, "We've seen lots of miracles that I don't have time to share. But there is one thing I can tell you for sure: those miracles never would have happened if life had gone according to my old script."

Anti-Miracles

Have you ever prayed for something and instead of getting the answer you asked for, you get the exact opposite? I call it an anti-answer to prayer. And it has happened to me more than once! In fact, it happened twice with the same prayer.

During the early days of National Community Church, the church office was a spare bedroom in our house. Then when our daughter, Summer, was born, it became her bedroom by night and the church office by day. The commute was amazing, but it got real old real fast. NCC was meeting in the movie theaters at Union Station, so we decided to look for a row house in that neighborhood that we could convert into a church office.

We found the perfect place, twice. The layout and location were absolutely ideal, and so was the price. We laid claim to those properties in prayer, but both of them were sold out from under us the night before the day we presented our offer! It was like a sucker punch followed by a sucker punch. My faith was so deflated I stopped looking. Then one day, a few weeks later, I was walking by 205 F Street NE—a row house one block from Union Station. The only downside was that it was right next to a crack house, but that downside was its upside. We had no idea at the time we purchased 205 F Street NE that the crack house would become Ebenezer's coffeehouse. But God knew. And that's why He closed the door on those other two properties.

Here's a lesson I've learned the hard way: you can't claim half a promise. We love asking God to open doors, a la Revelation 3:8–9. But it's disingenuous asking God to open a door if you aren't willing to let Him close a door. Those closed doors would prove to be trapdoors if we walked through them—they would take us places we don't want to go. When God closes a door, it often seems like an anti-miracle. But what seems to be a setback is God setting you up for something bigger, something better. If we had not purchased 205 F Street NE, we would have never been able to pull off our coffeehouse construction project. What seemed like a double fail turned into a double miracle—205 *and* 201 F Street NE.

The Glory of God

A few months ago a friend of mine was diagnosed with cancer, and we've been praying for spontaneous remission—the medical term for miracle. Unfortunately, further tests were trending in the wrong direction at his first follow-up visit. When my friend called me, it was tough to know what to say. And the truth is, it's better to listen than to talk. But then I felt like I needed to remind him of a simple yet difficult truth: "I'm going to keep praying for your healing, but healing isn't the ultimate goal. The ultimate goal is God's glory."

I'd love for God to glorify Himself by healing my friend, but even if my friend is healed, that wasn't the ultimate goal. The goal isn't the miracle. The goal is God's glory. And if you forget that, it's difficult to get through difficult circumstances. So let me offer this reminder: the will of God is the glory of God. That's why cancer can't keep you from doing the will of God. Nothing can. You can glorify God under any and every circumstance.

As a parent, I want to protect my kids from pain and suffering, but sometimes pain and suffering can have a sanctifying effect on our kids. So if our goal is that God would glorify Himself through our kids, then we can't pray away every problem. I'm certainly not suggesting that we don't protect our kids or pray a hedge of protection around them. But it's a false assumption to think that the will of God is an insurance plan. It's a dangerous plan. Just read Hebrews 11:

> I do not have time to tell about Gideon, Barak, Samson and Jephthah, about David and Samuel and the prophets, who through faith conquered kingdoms, administered justice, and gained what was promised; who shut the mouths of lions, quenched the fury of the flames, and escaped the edge of the sword; whose weakness was turned to strength; and who became powerful in battle and routed foreign armies. Women received back their dead, raised to life again.[6]

I wish the chapter ended there. It doesn't.

> There were others who were tortured, refusing to be released so that they might gain an even better resurrection. Some faced jeers and flogging, and even chains and imprisonment. They were put to death by stoning; they were sawed in two; they were killed by the sword. They went about in sheepskins and goatskins, destitute, persecuted and mistreated—the world was not worthy of them.[7]

Were only half of them in the will of God? The ones who conquered kingdoms or shut the mouths of lions? Or were all of them in the will of God—including the ones who were sawed in two?

The will of God isn't safe. In fact, it might even get you killed. But if God gets the glory, then the goal is accomplished. And the eternal reward we receive will be well worth any sacrifices we make.

If you think of the will of God in temporal terms, it doesn't add up. You've got to add eternity into the equation. And if my friend isn't healed until he reaches the other side of the space-time continuum, it'll be no less miraculous then than it would be now.

You'll Get Through This

Right before he released his thirtieth title, *You'll Get Through This*, we had the privilege of hosting Max Lucado at National Community Church. Max shared a story about his friend JJ Jasper, whose five-year-old son, Cooper, was killed in a dune buggy crash.[8] What started out as a carefree father-son outing turned into tragedy when the buggy flipped over, and Cooper died just hours later. And JJ's grief was coupled with guilt because he was the driver.

After calling 911, JJ then had to call his wife and share the news. Before making the call, the Holy Spirit gave him the words to say, just as He promised He would do during life's most difficult moments. JJ said, "I've got some bad news to share, but before I tell you, I want you to think about everything that you know that is good about God."

After witnessing his friend walk through this dark night of the soul, Max decided to do exactly what JJ prescribed. He knew he might need that checklist someday too. So Max quarried the Bible for the goodness of God. Here's a short list he came up with, and it's helped him get through many of the trials he's faced:

> God is still sovereign no matter what. He still knows my name. Angels still respond to his call. The hearts of rulers still bend at his bidding. The death of Jesus still saves souls. The Spirit of God still indwells saints. Heaven is still only heartbeats away. The grave is still temporary housing. God is still faithful. He is not caught off guard. He uses everything for his glory and my ultimate good. He uses tragedy to accomplish his will and his will is right, holy, and perfect. Sorrow may come with the night, but joy comes with the morning.[9]

While the Bible reveals very little about the parents of the man born blind, it's not hard to imagine the bitter disappointment of discovering that their son would never see them with his physical eyes. It was emotional whiplash unlike anything they had ever experienced. And the unanswered questions would haunt them the rest of their lives. In those moments, all you can do is fall on the grace of God with your full weight.

That's exactly what JJ did. And that's what got him through the most difficult chapter in his life. In JJ's words, "People with good intentions say time heals all wounds. That's not true. You'll never get over it. When you lose a loved one you care deeply about, you'll never get over it, but you will get through it."[10]

Why do children fall out of windows?

Why do kids die in dune buggy accidents?

Why are babies born blind?

Those are unanswerable questions. Those are questions we take to the grave with us. But you can't let the questions you cannot answer keep you from trusting what you know to be true.

God is good, all the time. All the time, God is good.

In the words of Corrie ten Boom, "There is no pit too deep that God's grace isn't deeper still."[11] Those words are not clichés. They were coupled with Corrie's memories of the Nazi concentration camp where she was imprisoned during World War II. It was through the cinematic portrayal of her miraculous survival in the 1975 Billy Graham film *The Hiding Place* that I first encountered the grace of God. The same grace that enabled Corrie to survive hell on earth helped punch my ticket to heaven.

Explanatory Style

In his book *Learned Optimism*, Dr. Martin Seligman hypothesizes that all of us have what he calls an "explanatory style" to account for life's experiences. In his words, "Explanatory style is the manner in which you habitually explain to yourself why events happen."[12]

Let's say you're at a restaurant waiting for a date that you were supposed to meet at 7:00 sharp, but forty-five minutes later he or she is a no-show. At some point you need to explain to yourself why the person isn't there. Here are some possible explanations. You might think, "He stood me up," causing you to become mad. You could jump to conclusions and think, "She doesn't love me anymore," causing you to become sad. You could assume, "He was in an accident," causing you to feel anxious. You might imagine, "He's working overtime so that he can pay for our meal," causing you to feel grateful. You could speculate, "She's with another man," causing you to feel jealous. Or you might realize, "This gives me a perfect excuse to break up with her," giving you a great deal of relief.

Same situation.

Very different explanations.

There are lots of different explanations for every experience. And while you cannot control your experiences, you can control your explanations. Biblically speaking, your explanations are more important than your experiences. When bad things happen to us, it's easy to play the victim card. But you are not a victim. You are more than a conqueror![13]

If anybody had the right to have a victim mentality, it was Joseph. Everything that could go wrong did go wrong. He was betrayed by his brothers, sold into slavery, and falsely accused of a crime he did not commit. But after seventeen years of trials and tribulations, he reveals the explanatory style that got him through the tough times:

> You intended to harm me, but God intended it for good to accomplish what is now being done, the saving of many lives.[14]

Bitter or better? It depends upon your explanatory style.

In the words of Aldous Huxley, "Experience is not what happens to you; it is what you do with what happens to you."[15]

A few years ago a college cheerleader hobbled into church on crutches. When I asked her what happened, she could barely hold back the tears. She had torn her Achilles tendon, had to have surgery to repair it, and was in a cast for eight weeks. Four days after getting her cast off, she re-tore the same tendon stepping on a patch of ice and had to have a second surgery. The reinjury was devastating, but God used her rehab to resurrect her dream of becoming an athletic trainer. While she would have rather studied the subject in a textbook, she realized that God was giving her a graduate degree! It was a tough test, but she aced the exam with her explanatory style.

I don't know why bad things happen to good people or why good things happen to bad people. But I do know this: "in all things God works for the good of those who love him, who have been called according to his purpose."[16] And if you allow Him, He'll recycle your pain for someone else's gain.

If you dare to do a double take, you'll discover that some of life's greatest miracles look like complete disasters at first glance.

The Second Half

As a pastor, I'm confronted by the raw reality of sin and suffering on a regular basis. Sometimes it's a seemingly unbearable burden, like the death of a child. Other times it's an unconscionable decision, like an affair. And while the weight of sin and suffering feels like the weight of the world, I'm amazed at those whose Herculean faith is resilient enough to bear up under life's most difficult predicaments.

Kim Green is one of those heroes.

When bad news is delivered in a hospital delivery room, it can turn one of life's most joyous occasions into a parent's worst nightmare. Kim's dream is to minister to those parents who walk through that nightmare. She adopts babies with terminal issues. Kim knows that these children won't live long lives, but she loves them as much as she can for as long as she can.

One of Kim's fourteen adopted children was a little girl named Selah Hope, who was conceived in rape. Born with no brain, just a brain stem, Selah lived only fifty-five days. But in Kim's words, "Every life has a purpose." Even Selah's. Kim not only cared for her adopted daughter during her short life, but she also loved her Muslim birth mother. And it was Kim's tangible love that led this woman to faith in Jesus Christ. Why Jesus didn't heal Selah is a mystery to me. But is it possible that she fulfilled her purpose? There is nothing good about the circumstances surrounding her birth. But God can take the worst life has to offer and use it for eternal purposes.

That doesn't mean that your deepest hurts are healed or that your hardest questions are answered. Time does not heal all wounds, but eternity will. You might end up with more questions than answers, just like the man born blind. But if you give God half a chance, He'll give you a second chance. And while the man born blind couldn't get back the first half of his life, I'm guessing he enjoyed the second half twice as much.

21

SPIT ON IT

He spit on the ground, made some mud with the saliva, and
put it on the man's eyes.

John 9:6

SHORTLY AFTER MOVING to Washington, DC, I took Lora
to a performance of the National Symphony Orchestra
at the Kennedy Center. All I remember from that experience
is the guy sitting next to me. I almost went deaf in my left
ear! This guy got up out of his seat and gave the conductor
a standing ovation before the orchestra even started playing!
That's when I knew it was going to be a very long concert. Mr.
Symphony kept yelling, "Bravo!" And I mean *yelling*, because
we were in the third balcony! When I go to a football game,
I expect some crazed fans, but at the symphony? His hands
had to be black-and-blue the next day from all his clapping.

Throughout the entire performance I kept thinking, *Are
we even listening to the same symphony?* By the end of the

night I concluded that we were indeed listening to the same orchestra, but we were *hearing* two very different symphonies!

An old proverb says, "Those who hear not the music, think the dancer mad."

Again, it's not just beauty that is in the eye of the beholder. Everything is. And it's not just the eye; it's the ear too.

We don't experience the world as it is. We experience the world *as we are*. Our outer reality eventually becomes a mirror reflection of our inner reality.

An experiment involving a group of Americans who had never been to Mexico and a group of Mexicans who had never been to America proves the point. The researchers built a binocular viewing machine capable of showing one image to the right eye and one image to the left eye. One of the snapshots was of a baseball game, a traditional American pastime. The other photo was of a bullfight, a traditional Mexican pastime. During the experiment, the pictures appeared simultaneously, forcing subjects to focus on one or the other. When asked what they had seen, the American subjects reported seeing a baseball game, while their Mexican counterparts reported seeing a bullfight.[1]

How we perceive the world around us largely depends upon what we've experienced or not experienced, what we know or don't know, what we expect or don't expect. That is why Americans see a baseball game while Mexicans see a bullfight. That's also why the Pharisees missed the miracle that happened right in front of their eyes!

Dominant Eye

A few years ago I took my son Parker to shoot clay pigeons for his birthday. I'd never shot a gun, so I had to take a gun safety course before they'd let me on the range. And it's a good thing I did. Not just for safety reasons but for aiming reasons.

I don't know how I missed this memo my entire life, but did you know you have a dominant eye? Make a triangle with your hands, fully extend your arms, and find an object to focus on. Now close one eye, then the other. With one eye, the object will move—that's your weak eye. If you aim with that eye, you'll miss the target every time! But with your dominant eye, the object will stay in the triangle. I'm right-eyed, so I close my left eye to shoot.

I think many people are looking at life through their weak eye! If you have a critical eye, you'll find something wrong with everything. And that's exactly what the Pharisees did. They were so focused on the law, they couldn't see past it. And Jesus called them on it:

> For judgment I came into this world, that those who do not see may see, and those who see may be made blind.[2]

The irony of the sixth miracle is that the man born blind ends up with sight and the seeing Pharisees end up legally blind.

Faith isn't just a way of living.

Faith is also a way of seeing.

The old adage is true: seeing is believing. But the opposite is even truer: believing is seeing.

The Light of the World

Right before performing the sixth miracle, Jesus reveals one dimension of His true identity: "I am the light of the world."[3] The Pharisees rejected His claim because they said Jesus was bearing witness about Himself. So Jesus turned the man born blind into His eyewitness, literally.

The sixth miracle is a reflection of the original miracle—creation. In the beginning God said, "Let there be light."[4] God speaks, and the first sound waves don't just travel through space; they create it. Light waves defeat darkness at a rate of 186,000 miles per second.

Less than a century ago the prevailing opinion in cosmology was that the Milky Way galaxy was the sum total of the universe. Nineteenth-century Austrian physicist Christian Doppler had theorized an expanding universe, but there wasn't much tangible evidence to back up his belief. Then an astronomer named Edwin Hubble spied several spiral nebulae that were far too distant to be part of the Milky Way galaxy. The announcement of his discovery on January 1, 1925, was an astronomical paradigm shift. He discovered that the degree of redshift observed in light coming from other galaxies increased in proportion to the distance of that galaxy from the Milky Way. In other words, the universe is still expanding. The significance of that is this: the original "Let there be light" is still creating galaxies at the outer edges of the universe! Amazing thought, isn't it? Billions of galaxies trace their origin to four words.

Now let me ask you a question: If God can create billions of galaxies with four words, what can't He do?

The same voice that spoke order into chaos at the dawn of creation is still doing it. And He does it again with the man born blind. That man's world was not unlike the pre-creation world described in Genesis: "Darkness was over the face of the deep."[5] Then the same light that caused Genesis, caused synaptogenesis.

Ultrasound

Genesis 1:3 tells us, "And God said, 'Let there be light.'" When we hear the word *said*, we tend to think *linguistics*. But if you want to fully appreciate the first words of God, you need to think *physics*. Sound isn't just language. It is first and foremost a form of energy. In fact, the word *said* might be better translated *challenged* in the context of creation. God challenges the darkness. And darkness is defeated by light.

Scientifically speaking, the human voice is simply sound waves with different frequencies traveling through space at 1,125 feet per second. The vocal range for humans is between 55 and 880 hertz, and that means that our voices are pretty much good for one thing: communication. We use our voices to sing or shout or speak. But not God. God uses His voice to turn darkness into light, to turn chaos into created order.

Just as our vocal capacity is limited to a relatively small range between 55 and 880 hertz, so our range of hearing is limited to sound waves between 20 and 20,000 hertz. Anything below 20 hertz is infrasonic for humans. Anything above 20,000 hertz is ultrasonic. Anything outside that range is inaudible, but that is when the power of sound is truly revealed.

Infrasound has the capacity to cause headaches and earthquakes. According to zoologists, infrasound helps elephants predict changes in weather and helps birds navigate as they migrate. Infrasound can also be used to locate underground oil or predict volcanic eruptions. On the other end of the sound spectrum, ultrasound has the power to kill insects, track submarines, break glass, perform noninvasive surgery, topple buildings, clean jewelry, catalyze chemical reactions, heal damaged tissues, pasteurize milk, break up kidney stones, drill through hard materials, and of course give you the first glimpse of your unborn son or daughter via sonogram.

There is a lot more to sound than meets the ear!

I know people who claim they have never heard the voice of God. And that may be true, if we're referencing His audible voice. But you have *seen* His voice. Absolutely everything that exists is a visible echo of those four words: *Let there be light*.

God's ability to speak isn't limited to our ability to hear. God doesn't just use words to communicate; He uses His words to turn water into wine, make blind eyes see, and call dead people back to life. Like infrasonic and ultrasonic sound waves, His words are full of power, and they never return void. Evidently, His spit doesn't either!

Spit on It

After pronouncing Himself the light of the world, Jesus spit on the ground and made mud with His saliva. Then He anointed the man's eyes with it.[6]

I have several reactions to this part of the story. The first one is, *gross!* My secondary reaction is, *why?* Scholars have been debating that question for two millennia. Why does Jesus use spit to make mud?

In the Greco-Roman world, saliva was associated with magical powers. So the Pharisees would have had a negative reaction to this. Plus, it was illegal to make mud on the Sabbath. Honestly, I wonder if Jesus was just pushing their buttons again. While I'm not sure of the motivation, Jesus does seem to be asserting His genesis power. He originally formed man from the dust of the earth—genesis.[7] Now He spits on the dust and makes mud to make blind eyes see— synaptogenesis. The One who created everything in the first place is the One who can re-create anything in the second place.

When it comes to miracles, be very careful about focusing on the methodology. If you do, lots of people will end up with mud in their eyes! The methodology behind the miracles of Jesus isn't the point. The point is His power.

There is nothing He cannot do. But once again, we have to do our part.

Go and Wash

Like many of the miracles Jesus performed, this one comes with a set of instructions. He tells the man to go and wash in the Pool of Siloam.[8] While we don't know the exact distance he traveled to get to the pool, it was a hike. I've actually hiked through Hezekiah's tunnel, which connects the Gihon Spring with the Pool of Siloam. The man born blind would have descended hundreds of steps, and this miracle happened during the Feast of Tabernacles, so he would have bumped into tens of thousands of pilgrims.

So why would Jesus send this blind man on a scavenger hunt? Why not just heal him on the spot? A trip to the Pool of Siloam seems unnecessary, doesn't it?

Hold that thought.

I recently heard a story told by an Episcopal bishop named William Frey.[9] As a young man, he volunteered to tutor a student who was blind. The student had lost his sight at the age of thirteen in a chemical explosion. He felt like his life was over. The only thing greater than his self-pity was his hatred toward God. For six months after the accident, all he did was feel sorry for himself. Then one day his father said, "John, winter's coming and the storm windows need to be up—that's your job. I want those hung by the time I get back this evening or else!" Then he pretended to walk out of the room, slamming the door. John got good and angry! In fact, he was so angry that he decided to do it. He thought, *When I fall, they'll have a blind and paralyzed son!* But John didn't fall. He discovered that he was capable of doing far more than he realized, even with blind eyes. Only after completing the job did he discover that his dad was never more than five feet away. He shadowed his son to make sure he was safe, but he knew that helplessness was a far worse curse than blindness.

I'm not entirely sure why Jesus had this blind man go and wash, but I'm guessing that he had lived a relatively helpless life. He depended upon everybody for everything! So Jesus didn't just heal his blind eyes. He restored his dignity by rebuking helplessness.

Scripture is explicit when it comes to the sequence of this miracle. It says he "came back seeing."[10] If he hadn't taken this step of faith and gone to the Pool of Siloam, I don't think the miracle would have happened! And that's one secret to experiencing the miraculous: *most miracles require an act of blind obedience.*

You cannot manufacture miracles, but you can wash in the Pool of Siloam.

One step of obedience can open your eyes.

One step of obedience can reverse the curse.

One step of obedience can begin a new chapter in your life!

THE SEVENTH SIGN

When Mary reached the place where Jesus was and saw him, she fell at his feet and said, "Lord, if you had been here, my brother would not have died."

When Jesus saw her weeping, and the Jews who had come along with her also weeping, he was deeply moved in spirit and troubled. "Where have you laid him?" he asked.

"Come and see, Lord," they replied.

Jesus wept.

Then the Jews said, "See how he loved him!"

But some of them said, "Could not he who opened the eyes of the blind man have kept this man from dying?"

Jesus, once more deeply moved, came to the tomb. It was a cave with a stone laid across the entrance. "Take away the stone," he said.

"But, Lord," said Martha, the sister of the dead man, "by this time there is a bad odor, for he has been there four days."

Then Jesus said, "Did I not tell you that if you believe, you will see the glory of God?"

So they took away the stone. Then Jesus looked up and said, "Father, I thank you that you have heard me. I knew that you always hear me, but I said this for the benefit of the people standing here, that they may believe that you sent me."

When he had said this, Jesus called in a loud voice, "Lazarus, come out!" The dead man came out, his hands and feet wrapped with strips of linen, and a cloth around his face.

Jesus said to them, "Take off the grave clothes and let him go."

John 11:32–44

22

THE GRAVE ROBBER

If you had been here, my brother would not have died. But
I know that even now God will give you whatever you ask.

John 11:21–22

ONE OF MY earliest movie memories is the 1978 version
of *Superman* starring Christopher Reeve. Superman's
heartthrob, Lois Lane, is driving through the Nevada desert
when a crevice opened by an earthquake swallows her car.
Superman can't get there in time to save Lois because he's
busy building a natural dam out of boulders to stop a flood
caused by a breach in the Hoover Dam. When he discovers
that Lois is dead, Superman gets super angry. He flies around
the earth at supersonic speeds, reversing its rotation, theoreti-
cally turning back time.

Now, I know the science behind that scene is suspect. After
all, the earth rotates around its axis at one thousand miles
per hour. So if Superman had reversed its rotation, he may

have saved Lois Lane, but everyone else on the planet would have died of whiplash! But it's still a cool concept, isn't it? Don't you wish you could turn back time right after saying or doing something you wish you hadn't? The problem, of course, is that the arrow of time points in one direction.

What's done is done. Some things in life are irreversible.

You cannot unbake cookies, uncut hair, undelete documents, or unrun red lights. These are a few of the lessons I've learned the hard way. Some of those lessons were easily laughed off after a little embarrassment—like the bald strip on the back of my head after the barber said, "Oops." I actually used Lora's mascara for a few weeks until the bald spot grew back out. Others cost me a little cash, like a $110 ticket for running a red light. Then there are those irreversible moments that leave a hole in your heart forever—like standing at the foot of my father-in-law's casket after a heart attack ended his earthly life at fifty-five years of age.

One of those painful lessons came during my sophomore basketball season in college. Not only did we lose our last game and bow out of the national tournament, but I also tore my anterior cruciate ligament in the fourth quarter. When the doctor gave me his diagnosis, I asked him when it would be healed. He said *never*. He told me I needed to have reconstructive surgery because torn ligaments don't heal. At that point in my life basketball *was* my life. So it felt like my life as I knew it was over.

If you've been on the receiving end of divorce papers, received a frantic phone call in the middle of the night, or gotten lab results from your doctor that affirm your worst fears, you know that feeling all too well. And that's precisely how Mary and Martha felt. Their brother was gone for good. And their lives as they knew them were over. But it's not over until God says it's over!

Jesus showed up four days late, but He showed off His power in a way never before witnessed. He had reversed withered arms and weather systems. But the seventh miracle was a sudden-death showdown with an undefeated opponent. The Grave Robber went toe-to-toe with death itself, and death met its match.

The Law of Entropy

The second law of thermodynamics states that if left to its own devices, everything in the universe moves toward disorder and decay. Cars rust. Food rots. And of course humans grow old and die. It takes many forms, but it's called the law of entropy. And the only way to prevent entropy is to introduce an outside energy source to counteract it. The technical term is negentropy, and the refrigerator is a perfect example. If you plug it into an electrical outlet, it produces cold air that keeps food from rotting. If, however, the refrigerator gets unplugged from its power source, entropy will take over again. This I know from personal experience. Our family returned from a Christmas vacation and I knew something was wrong before we even walked in the front door. We were greeted by a dead refrigerator that smelled like a dead animal. Word to the wise: if your refrigerator dies, keep its door closed.

While we're on the subject of bad odors, that was Mary and Martha's greatest concern when Jesus told the mourners to roll away the stone. They were afraid it would stink to high heaven, but Jesus was about to counteract four days of decomposition with one miracle of negentropy.

The law of entropy doesn't just govern the physical universe. It has governed the spiritual realm since it was introduced in the Garden of Eden after Adam and Eve's original

235

sin. They had been forewarned: "You must not eat from the tree of the knowledge of good and evil, for when you eat from it you will certainly die."[1] While they didn't die immediately after eating the forbidden fruit, their disobedience introduced the process of decay that leads to physical and spiritual death. Sin is a slow-acting poison. Its immediate effects are often indiscernible, but the aftereffects are far more devastating than what we realize at the time. Original sin caused a disturbance in the Force, so to speak. It introduced sickness and suffering to the equation of life. Everything from genetic defects to natural disasters trace their origins back to original sin. We live in a fallen world—everything is affected by entropy.

Just like Adam and Eve discovered, sin opens the door to entropy. The more you sin, the more your life moves toward disorder and decay. Sin is much more than a moral dividing line between right and wrong. It's a matter of life and death. Jesus didn't die on the cross just to make bad people good. He brings dead people to life! And Lazarus is exhibit A.

Do the Lazarus

To fully appreciate the seventh miracle, you need a basic understanding of ancient Jewish burial traditions. When Lazarus died, his feet would have been bound at the ankles and his arms would have been tied to his body with linen strips. Then his dead body would have been wrapped in approximately one hundred pounds of graveclothes to protect and preserve the body. Some scholars believe that the head itself would have been wrapped with so many linens that it would measure a foot wide. So the best mental image is probably the one that immediately comes to mind—Lazarus looked like a mummy.

Based on Jewish burial traditions, it seems to me like two miracles happen here, not one. The first one is resurrection.

But how in the world did Lazarus get up and get out of the tomb in a full-body cast? That's the second miracle! I'm not sure I can re-create the scene, but Lazarus did not walk out of the tomb. I think he hopped out.

> The dead man came out, his hands and feet wrapped with strips of linen, and a cloth around his face.[2]

Maybe my imagination gets a little carried away, but I bet his friends and family "did the Lazarus" at dance parties every chance they got. Lazarus had to bust a move to get out of that tomb. And once again, Jesus turns tragedy into comedy. When Lazarus comes hopping out of the tomb, grieving turns to laughing. And they laughed about it the rest of their lives.

Now let me get serious. If you miss this, you miss the point. This miracle doesn't just foreshadow Jesus' own resurrection. It foreshadows yours! It's not just something Jesus did for Lazarus. It's a snapshot of what Jesus wants to do in your life right here, right now. When we sin, it's like the enemy of our soul wraps us up in graveclothes. Sin buries us alive and makes a mummy out of us. We become a shadow of the person we were meant to be. And if you keep on sinning, it'll weigh you down like a hundred pounds of graveclothes. But Jesus is calling you out of your tomb.

I've found that one of the best ways to personalize the promises in Scripture is to take out the original name and insert your own. And I think it's okay to do that. After all, every promise God has made is *yes* in Christ.[3] So take out Lazarus's name and insert your own: *Mark, come out!*

Can you hear Him call your name?

He's calling you out of sin.

He's calling you out of death.

He's calling you out of your tomb.

Second Life

Church tradition offers two versions of what happened to Lazarus after his resurrection. One holds that he and his sisters made their way to the island of Cyprus, where Lazarus was the first bishop of Kition. The Church of Saint Lazarus, in the modern city of Larnaca, is believed by some to be built over his second tomb, which he was buried in some thirty years after his first death. A second church tradition holds that Lazarus and his sisters ended up in Marseille, France, where Lazarus survived the persecution of Christians by Nero by hiding in a tomb, appropriately enough, but eventually died by beheading during the persecution ordered by Emperor Domitian.[4]

I'm not sure which tradition is true or if either of them is. But either way, Jesus gave Mary and Martha their brother back, and Lazarus lived two lives. How long he lived after he died, we don't know for sure. But Jesus gave him a second chance, a second life. And the Grave Robber wants to do for you what He did for Lazarus. But He doesn't just want to give back the life that sin and Satan have stolen. He came that you might have life and have it more abundantly![5] The Son of God entered space-time so that you could exit it—so that you could spend eternity with Him in a place where there is no more mourning or crying or pain. Heaven is the end of entropy as we know it, and death is defeated once and for all. In the words of the apostle Paul:

> Where, O death, is your victory?
> Where, O death, is your sting?[6]

When my father-in-law died, Parker and Summer were so young that they can't now remember him. So we would often tell stories to help create some memories for our kids.

During one of those conversations, Parker said, "I wish I could have said good-bye to Grandpa and told him to say hi to Jesus." In an overly excited voice, Summer responded, "When we die, we'll get to go to heaven and see Grandpa Schmidgall." To which Parker replied, "You shouldn't get so excited about dying!"

At first that was nothing more than a cute conversation that Lora and I cherished. But over the years I've realized that it's more than that. Remember when Jesus said we must become like little children? I think this is one dimension of that. At some point, the fear of death allays our anticipation of eternal life. But if you've already died to self, you don't have to fear death. You no longer have to live as if the purpose of life is to arrive safely at death.

There is nothing wrong with wanting to live a long life, but death isn't something we dread. Death was defeated two thousand years ago. And to be absent from the body is to be present with the Lord.[7] So death is something we can actually anticipate because it's not the end. It's a new beginning. And many of the miracles we hoped for on earth will finally be fulfilled in heaven.

Our second life begins when Christ calls us out of the tomb of sin. Our eternal life begins when our body is finally buried six feet deep. Death is the exit toll all of us must pay, but it's the entrance ramp to eternity.

23

EVEN NOW

Lazarus has died, and for your sake I am glad that I was not there.

John 11:14–15 ESV

I T RANKS AS one of the most embarrassing moments of my life. It's one thing to forget a wedding you're supposed to attend. It's another thing to forget a wedding you're supposed to officiate! Maybe it's because we didn't do a rehearsal the night before, but it totally slipped my mind.

Have you ever had a phone call trigger your memory? Like an alarm, the ring reminds you of something you were supposed to do or someplace you were supposed to be. The moment my phone rang, my stomach was in my throat because I remembered the noon wedding I was supposed to officiate. It was one o'clock and I was in a dressing room at the mall. I died a thousand deaths in that dressing room! The bride and groom started worrying about their no-show pastor around quarter to noon, but it took more than an hour to track down my cell phone number. And how they got it is nothing short of miraculous. They called the church office, but we're closed on Saturdays. Somehow the call got transferred to the emergency phone in the elevator at Ebenezer's coffeehouse, and it answered automatically. Our pastor of discipleship, Heather Zempel, happened to be on the elevator when the call came in. She actually thought it was a crank call because she couldn't imagine me forgetting a wedding, but I was guilty as charged.

I showered like Speedy Gonzales, threw on a suit like Superman, and drove to the wedding venue like it was the NASCAR Sprint Cup Series. I arrived at 3:00 sharp, and the ceremony commenced. It wasn't easy making eye contact with the wedding guests, but the bride and groom were unbelievably gracious. In fact, they still attend our church. Don't tell me miracles don't happen!

When I finally got there, I decided not to say what Jesus said when He was late to Lazarus's funeral. I did *not* say, "For your sake, I am glad I was not there."[1]

Why on earth would Jesus say that?

It seems thoughtless at best and heartless at worst. If your friend is on his deathbed and you have the ability to heal him, don't you drop everything and get there as quickly as possible? Yet Jesus stays put for two days. Then He takes His sweet time getting there. And the question is, *why?*

Passive-Aggressive

When Jesus finally shows up four days late, Mary and Martha get a little passive-aggressive with him. They both say the same exact thing: "If you had been here, my brother would not have died."[2] They aren't really blaming Jesus . . . but they are, but they aren't, but they are. And the truth is, we all have passive-aggressive tendencies toward God, don't we? We don't blame Him for the bad things that happen, but we also know He could have kept them from happening. So why doesn't He?

Why wouldn't Jesus just teleport to Bethany and heal Lazarus?

My take is this: Jesus had been there and done that. Jesus could have walked across water, arrived in the nick of time, and healed Lazarus as he was drawing his last breath. But Jesus had already revealed His healing power. It was time to unveil His *resurrection power.*

You cannot resurrect what has not died. So Jesus waited a little longer to reveal a little more of His power. And He does the same thing with us. If you feel like you're in a holding pattern, it may be because God is getting ready to do something more miraculous than you've previously experienced. But something precious might have to die first so that He can resurrect it.

If Jesus had simply healed Lazarus, I'm sure some people would have praised God. I'm also sure some skeptics would have claimed he wasn't really that sick to begin with or credited his recovery to the miracle of medicine. But when someone has been dead for four days, there is only one logical and theological explanation. You have witnessed a miracle of the first order, and that first-order miracle is the seventh sign in John's Gospel.

If Jesus had simply healed Lazarus, it would have reinforced the faith they already had. Jesus wanted to stretch their faith. And in order to do that, sometimes things have to go from bad to worse before they get better!

God's Grammar

I've forgotten most of the sermons I've heard, and I'm sure our congregation has forgotten most of mine. But every once in a while, there is a moment of revelation in the middle of a message that is life altering. That's what I experienced listening to an old sermon by Dr. Charles Crabtree titled "God's Grammar." I found one little line to be absolutely unforgettable: "Never put a comma where God puts a period and never put a period where God puts a comma."

When someone dies, we naturally put a period on it. Game over. But Jesus knew He would take it into overtime with a Hail Mary, so to speak. When He heard the news that Lazarus was sick, Jesus made a bold prediction: "This sickness will not end in death."[3] I used to have a problem with that statement because it seems like Jesus is wrong, right? After all, Lazarus does in fact die. But the operative word is *end*. Jesus said the sickness would not end in death, and it didn't. He knew Lazarus would die, but Jesus didn't put a period there. He inserted a four-day comma.

"Sometimes it looks like God is missing the mark," observed Oswald Chambers, "because we're too short-sighted to see what He's aiming for."[4]

Have you ever felt like God was a day late and a dollar short?

Mary and Martha felt like He was four days late! The window of opportunity closed when Lazarus drew his last breath, but it's not over until God says it's over! God always gets the final word. And Martha knew it. What comes out of her mouth ranks as one of the greatest statements of faith in all of Scripture:

> Lord . . . if you had been here, my brother would not have died. But I know that even now God will give you whatever you ask.[5]

Did you catch the conjunction? There is a *but* between her statement of fact and her statement of faith.

Evidently, Martha is still holding out hope four days after the funeral. To be honest, a psychotherapist might diagnose this as a psychotic break. After all, denial ain't just a river in Egypt. At what point do you stop hoping and start grieving? Day one? Day two? Day four? Some would say it was her grief speaking, but she was speaking out of *faith*. Faith often looks like it's out of touch with reality, but that's because it's in touch with a reality that is more real than anything you can see or hear or taste or touch or smell with your five senses. Faith is our sixth sense. And if you're truly in touch with God, sometimes it'll appear as if you are out of touch with reality.

The sentence should end after Martha says, "Lord, if you had been here my brother would not have died." But Martha doesn't put a period there. Faith inserts a comma, even at the end of a death sentence. That's what Martha does: "Even now God will give you whatever you ask."

I love the little phrase embedded in this statement of faith: *even now*. It's one of my favorite phrases in all of Scripture. Even when it seems like God is four days late, it's too soon to give up. Even when it seems like your dream is dead and buried, don't put a period there.

Here Comes the Boom

Susanna Wright and her husband minister in one of the poorest areas of London. During a difficult season of ministry, Susanna lost the very hope she offered. And it was compounded by the fact that her dream of having her book published was all but dead. In her words, "I forgot about the resurrection." And the same thing happens to us, doesn't it? Many Christians remember the resurrection once a year! The rest of the year we live as if Jesus is still nailed to the cross.

When Susanna hit bottom, she picked up a copy of *The Circle Maker*, and God resurrected her writing dream. Like so many aspiring authors, Susanna didn't know a single soul in the publishing industry. So breaking into that industry felt like breaking into Buckingham Palace.

One day Susanna was scouring the website of an international publishing house when she discovered that their UK office was in London, just two miles from her home. She decided to circle their office building every week, praying for a way in. Week in and week out, Susanna prayed morning, noon, and night. Then one morning she threw down the gauntlet with God. She said, "Lord, I'm sick of praying day and night for a breakthrough. I want to feel the boom that Mark Batterson talks about."

Susanna was referencing the part in *The Circle Maker* where I shared the science behind a sonic boom and likened it to the breakthrough we experience when we pray through. Almost like a sonic boom, there comes a moment in prayer when you know that God has answered your prayer. While the answer may not be a physical reality yet, you know it's just a matter of time before God delivers on His promise.

Just as Susanna prayed for that boom, a London double-decker drove up, painted with a bus-size billboard that simply said, "Here comes the boom!" Susanna started laughing out loud as people stood and stared at her. Once she regained her composure, Susanna took a picture of the bus and hung it in her kitchen. Shortly thereafter, the publisher Susanna had been circling in prayer offered to publish her book. She says:

> All my life, I have written. I wrote my first poem at seven; sent off my first story to a children's publisher when I was eleven; and now, I will be a published writer. I have experienced a revival I did not think possible in my heart. God has somehow set my life right again. He has opened the doors of a major

publishing house and launched a writing ministry that has been brewing in me for nearly three decades.

When it comes to God-ordained dreams, I can almost guarantee that they will take longer and be harder to accomplish than you ever imagined. By definition, a God-ordained dream will always be beyond your ability and beyond your resources. But that is how God gets the glory. If you feel like your dream is dead and buried, maybe God has you right where He wants you. Almost every dream I've ever had has gone through a death and resurrection. It's the litmus test. If it's not from God, it'll stay dead. If it is, it'll rise again. But you need to pray through until you experience the breakthrough.

Here comes the boom!

Not Yet

When God says no to a prayer, it doesn't always mean no. Sometimes it means *not yet*. It's the right request but the wrong time.

A few years ago Lora and I were house hunting on Capitol Hill. We had lived on the Hill since 1996 when we were fortunate enough to buy a hundred-year-old home during a buyer's market. As our kids got bigger, our fifteen-foot-wide row home got smaller, so we started looking for a little more elbow room. We found our dream home less than a block away.

Lora and I decided to make an offer, but we also knew our financial limits. After praying about it, we came up with our best offer and felt like it was a fleece. If God wanted us to have the house, the owner would accept our offer. With the real estate market lagging and the time on the market mounting, we were confident the seller would accept our offer. He did not. And as much as we wanted the house, and as tempted as we were to go beyond our predetermined offer, we made the difficult decision to walk away. And we stopped looking at homes.

One night about a year later, as we drove by the home we had tried to purchase, Lora said, "Do you ever feel like that is the one that got away?" We had driven by it a hundred times since the owner rejected our offer, and we had never said so much as a word about it. It was dead to us. But Lora's casual comment must have been a prophetic prayer, because the very next morning there was a For Sale sign in the yard. That's when I had a holy hunch that God's *no* a year earlier was really a *not yet*.

What Lora and I didn't know was that the owner had never sold the house. It sat on the market for 252 days with no buyer, so it was taken off the market. When the same owner put the house back on the market, we decided to make the same offer. It was a calculated risk because he'd already said no once, but it was another fleece. We told our real estate agent it was our first and final offer. We were willing to walk away a second time, but we didn't have to. God answered our prayer a full year after we thought He would.

Most miracles take longer than we want, but the longer we wait, the more we appreciate them. I hope your miracle doesn't take thirty-eight years like the invalid's, but no matter how long it takes, you need to trust God's timing. Miracles happen once we're good and ready, and not a moment sooner. Sometimes it's because God in His grace is allowing us to mature so we'll be able to steward it. Sometimes He waits so we don't miss the point. And sometimes God waits to punctuate His power.

Having gone through a death and resurrection with our dream home has made us appreciate it more than we would have otherwise. It also ensures that we own our house, not the other way around. When something is given back after it is taken away, whether it's a house or our health, we don't take it for granted. It's like having your cake and eating it too! In our case, God even put some icing on it. Because we waited a year to buy our new home, our old home actually went up in value by 10 percent because the real estate market in DC rebounded. So we got our new home for the same amount of money and sold our old house for a lot more money than we would have a year earlier! Tithing on the sale of our house was one of the easiest checks we've ever written because God's hand of favor was so evident.

Second-Degree Faith

Let me double back to Martha's statement of faith:

> Lord . . . if you had been here, my brother would not have died. But I know that even now God will give you whatever you ask.[6]

This one statement reveals two types of faith.

The first half is what I call *preventative faith*. Martha says, "Lord, if you had been here, my brother would not have died."[7] Preventative faith believes God can keep things from happening. So we pray for traveling mercies or a hedge of protection around our children. And while there is nothing wrong with that, there is a second dimension of faith that believes that God can actually undo what's been done. I call it *resurrection faith*. It's a faith that refuses to put periods at the end of disappointments because God can make your impossible possible. Even when the application is denied or the adoption falls through or the business goes bankrupt, you don't put a period there. Even then you believe *even now*.

At some point, most of us end up with a dream that is buried six feet under failure. In fact, that's true of nearly every dream God has ever given me!

When I was in college, I dreamed of planting a church and pastoring it for life. I've been living that dream for seventeen years as the lead pastor of National Community Church in Washington, DC, but there is a prequel. My first attempt was a complete failure. When I was in seminary, the dream of planting a church in Chicago turned into a nightmare. The good news is that when that dream died, part of my ego died with it. Few things kill pride faster than failure! And that's the point. God doesn't want to kill the dream He's given you, but He does want to crucify anything that would keep Him from getting all of the glory when you ultimately succeed.

There are times when you need to hang on to a dream for dear life, but there are also times when a dream needs to be laid to rest. And it takes discernment to know the difference. I suppose Mary and Martha could have kept Lazarus lying in state on his deathbed instead of embalming him and laying him in the tomb. But their human attempt to make a miracle easier would have actually robbed God of the opportunity to reveal His resurrection power! It's one thing raising the dead off of their deathbed. It's another thing calling a dead man out of a tomb four days postmortem!

What needs to die so that it can be resurrected? So that God can reveal more of His power? So that God gets all of the glory?

You need to bury it.

Then if it's resurrected, you know God did it.

It takes courage to end an unhealthy dating relationship, but you won't find Mr. Right as long as you are dating Mr. Wrong. It takes courage to quit a job, but it might be the difference between making a living and making a life. It takes courage to change majors, but it's better to fail at something you love than succeed at something you hate. Maybe you need to bury the relationship, bury the job, or bury the major. Then you need to wait for Jesus to show up.

Over the past year and a half, I've prayed for someone in our church who felt called to quit his job during a forty-day prayer challenge. After filling out more than 330 job applications with no offers, he second-guessed his decision more than a time or two. Faith turned to doubt, then doubt turned to depression. "Turns out my forty-day prayer challenge went into overtime!" he told me. More like double overtime! Then, just when he felt as if he was unemployable, he beat out fifty other applicants for his dream job. "I don't know why I had a seventeen-month time-out," he confessed. "But since I'm single, my career was by far the most important thing in my life. Maybe that's why God took it away temporarily."

When God takes something away from us, it doesn't always mean that He takes it away forever. In fact, God often takes things away with the express purpose of giving them back. And when He does, we're able to see the miracle for what it is. If you've lost love and found it again, you know whereof I speak. The same is true of health and wealth. It's much more difficult to take the blessing for granted.

Jesus Wept

It was customary in ancient Israel to bury someone on the day of death. After death, the Talmud prescribed seven days of deep mourning and thirty days of light mourning. So Jesus shows up right in the middle of their deepest sorrow and grieves with them. John 11:35 simply says:

> Jesus wept.

It's one of the shortest verses in the Bible, but it speaks volumes. And I'm not sure the English translation does it justice. The force of the Greek verb tense suggests that Jesus burst into tears. This was no measured response. Jesus literally lost it. It reveals how much Jesus loved Lazarus. It also reveals a God who sheds tears! And He doesn't just cry over us, He collects our tears in a bottle.[8]

Your tears are precious to God. Whether they are tears of joy, tears of sorrow, or tears of pain—not one teardrop is lost on God.

If you've endured the type of loss Mary and Martha experienced, you know that sometimes you just need a shoulder to cry on. I'm grateful for those friends who seem to show up when everybody else disappears. Jesus is a friend who sticks closer than a brother,[9] and His broad shoulders can bear any burden. But sometimes you need more than a listening ear, more than a shoulder to cry on. You need a friend *who can do something about your situation.* The good news is: Jesus is both.

Jesus doesn't just get sad. The Son of God gets mad. Death was never part of God's original plan. It was the fallout from the fall. Jesus is good and angry because death has stolen His friend. So the Grave Robber steals him back!

24

RISK YOUR REPUTATION

Jesus, once more deeply moved, came to the tomb. It was a cave with a stone laid across the entrance. "Take away the stone," he said.

"But, Lord," said Martha, the sister of the dead man, "by this time there is a bad odor, for he has been there four days."

John 11:38–39

WHEN HE WAS twenty-five years old, evangelist Clayton King led a fifty-mile backpacking trip into the Himalaya mountains to share the gospel with an unreached people group in the Zanskar Valley.[1] Along with the physical challenge of making the mountainous hike, the risk of being kidnapped or killed was very real. Just a few months before their trip, a group of European missionaries were executed by Islamic militants for attempting to smuggle eleven Bibles across the border. Clayton and his friends had *eleven hundred* Bibles in their backpacks!

In preparation for their missionary journey, the team did water-only fasts, trained with weighted backpacks, and read as much as they could about Tibetan Buddhism. One of the team members was a doctor, so they manufactured a mobile medical clinic to take with them. And last but not least, they prayed for miracles, because they knew they'd need them. Lots of them.

The five-person team flew into Leh, one of the highest airports in the world. After acclimating to the 11,000-foot elevation, they traveled along the Kashmiri border with Pakistan toward the remote village of Zangla. On the way there, one divine appointment set the tone for the rest of the trip. In the middle of nowhere, they came across a hitchhiker who was standing by the side of the road. For all they knew, this man could be a terrorist, so the team protested when their native-born driver pulled over to pick him up. Clayton objected so vehemently that the hitchhiker said in his broken English, "You are a very loud-talking boy." Then he revealed why the driver stopped: "My name is Raja Norbu, and I am the king of the Zanskar Valley. I live in a small village called Zangla. It is very far from here and difficult to reach. As provincial governor, I must attend annual meetings in the capital of Delhi. I was on my way there when my vehicle broke down. Your driver recognized me as King Norbu."

What are the odds?

I don't know about you, but I've met exactly zero kings! And Clayton didn't just meet a king, he met the king of the very village his team was trying to reach!

Sometimes God shows up. Sometimes God shows off.

After revealing who he was, the king of Zangla asked Clayton's name. When he replied, "Clayton King," King Norbu took him literally! When he asked why an American king would visit his village, Clayton didn't pull any punches. He told the king that they wanted to set up a medical clinic and give his people copies of their holy book, the Bible. King Norbu was so pleased that he gave Clayton a handwritten letter that not only ensured safe passage and a warm reception in Zangla but also named Clayton the interim king while he was away. So when the team arrived in Zangla, they were treated like, you guessed it, kings!

A Show of Power

The second day in the village, the queen asked Clayton if he knew how to deliver a baby. Clayton had no clue, but the medical doctor on their team certainly did. She examined the mother and her twin babies, quickly assessing the situation. It was a high-risk pregnancy to begin with, but to complicate matters, the first baby was breech. And in the doctor's professional opinion, the baby had already died in utero.

Clayton isn't sure what came over him in that moment, but he asked his interpreter to translate a message. It wasn't until after the words were already out of his mouth that he realized the potential ramifications. With the boldness of an Old Testament prophet, Clayton said:

> We have come from America as the people of God. Our God is Jesus Christ, who was killed for our sins and then raised from the dead. He's powerful and loving, and He will show you His power. This mother will live tonight. And these babies will live tonight. God has sent us to you for this purpose. If they die, then you can do with us anything you wish.

In order to deliver the baby who was in a breech position, the doctor had to break his hip. While that enabled the baby to be born, he was in fact stillborn. There was no pulse, no heartbeat, and no breath. They didn't know how long the baby had been dead, but Clayton did the only thing he knew how to do. He cried out to God like his life depended on it, and there was a good chance that his life did depend on it. The next few minutes proved to be the most poignant moments of Clayton's life. After what felt like four days, the Grave Robber did it again. God raised the dead right in front of their eyes. This stillborn baby let out a scream that was music to their ears!

In cultures that are superstitious or animistic, God will often reveal Himself with what missiologists call "a show of power." The showdown between Elijah and the prophets of Baal in 1 Kings 18 is a great example. It was like a prophetic cage fight with no holds barred. There was even some smack talk! And just as God proved His superior power to Baal worshipers, He proved His power to a village of Tibetan Buddhists by raising a baby from the dead.

Come Out

If you've read the Bible from cover to cover, you suffer from hindsight bias. You know how every story ends, so it's hard to imagine an alternate outcome. Not only do you lose the element of surprise, but you also lose the raw emotion. And that's certainly true of the seventh sign.

If you can, try to forget how this story ends. Now put yourself within earshot of Jesus when He says, "Lazarus, come out!"² You hear the words come out of His mouth, but you can hardly believe your ears!

Who talks to dead people as if they can hear you?

Who has the audacity to demand that the grave give up its dead?

Because we assume the outcome—Lazarus walking out of the tomb—we fail to appreciate the risk Jesus took. If

Lazarus remains dead, this ranks as Jesus' most embarrassing moment. And the family and friends who had gathered to grieve are the victims of a cruel joke!

Don't miss this little subplot in this story line.

The six miracles that precede this one certainly establish Jesus' credibility. He reveals His mastery over everything from water molecules to the four dimensions of space-time reality. But just like the world of athletics or entertainment, you're only as good as your last game or last performance. If Lazarus doesn't walk out of the tomb, Jesus' credibility is out the window. So when Jesus called Lazarus out, He was pushing all of His miraculous chips to the middle of the table and betting it all on Lazarus. The stakes could not have been any higher, but that's how most miracles happen.

The Hand of God

Do you know why most of us don't experience miracles? It's because we never put ourselves in situations that necessitate one! We comfort the grieving instead of calling dead people out of the tomb. But if we took a few more risks, we might see a few more miracles! And that's one more secret to experiencing the miraculous: *you have to risk your reputation.*

Sometimes you need to lay your credibility on the line! That's what Jesus did when He called Lazarus out of the tomb. That's what Clayton did when he proclaimed that those twin babies would live. And isn't that what Shadrach, Meshach, and Abednego did when they refused to bow down to a ninety-foot idol?[3]

They knew they'd be executed if they didn't bow down, but they feared God more than they feared death itself. They would rather die by the flame than dishonor God. So they defied the earthly king with a bold declaration:

King Nebuchadnezzar, we do not need to defend ourselves before you in this matter. If we are thrown into the blazing furnace, the God we serve is able to deliver us from it, and he will deliver us from Your Majesty's hand. But even if he does not, we want you to know, Your Majesty, that we will not serve your gods.[4]

To be honest, I could have come up with a dozen rationalizations to justify bowing down. "I'm bowing on the outside, but I'm not bowing on the inside." "I'll ask for forgiveness right after I get back up." "My fingers are crossed." "I'm only breaking one of the Ten Commandments." "What good am I to God if I'm dead?" When it comes to sinful rationalizations, we are infinitely creative, aren't we? But it's our rationalizations that often annul His miraculous intervention. When we compromise our integrity, we don't leave room for divine intervention. When we take matters into our own hands, we take God out of the equation. When we try to manipulate a situation, we miss out on the miracle.

Stop and think about it.

If Shadrach, Meshach, and Abednego had bowed down to the statue, they would have been delivered from the fiery furnace. But it would have been by the hand of man, not the hand of God. And while they would have saved their lives, they would have sacrificed their integrity. They also would have forfeited the miracle.

When we bow down to what's wrong, we put our reputation and God's reputation at risk. But when we stand up for what's right, we establish God's reputation by putting ourselves in a posture where God can show up and show off. And God does just that.

Not a hair on their heads was singed, and their clothing was not scorched. They didn't even smell of smoke![5]

A Double Miracle

I did a radio interview shortly after *The Circle Maker* released, and the host told me an amazing story about his missionary friend, Dr. Bob Bagley. Bob's church in Africa didn't have a church building, so they gathered under the shade of a single tree near the village. That is, until the local witch doctor cursed the tree. When it withered and died, the church didn't just lose their shade. They were overshadowed by the curse because it undermined the authority of their message.

Bob knew their status in the village was in jeopardy if he didn't do something about it, so he called for a public prayer meeting. Not unlike Elijah, who challenged the prophets of Baal to a prayer duel, Bob confronted the curse and called down a blessing on the tree that had died. He literally laid hands on the tree trunk and prayed that God would resurrect it.

It was a calculated risk, but every prayer is, isn't it? If God didn't answer Bob's prayer, he would have dug an even deeper hole! But if you don't ask for the miracle, you'll never know what God might have done. Again, God won't answer 100 percent of the prayers you don't pray. If you don't get the answer you prayed for, it's not a fail. After all, the answer is up to God. Prayer is the way we put the ball in God's court. The only way you can fail is by failing to ask.

Now having said that, let me say this: if you're going to call someone out of a tomb, you'd better make sure you heard from God. The same is true if you're going to lay hands on a tree or prophesy that a stillborn baby will live. But if God speaks, you'd better not remain silent.

Bob asked God to resurrect the tree, but I love the little tagline he added at the end of his prayer: "It's not my name that's at stake."

When you act in faith, it may seem like you are risking your reputation, but it's really God's reputation that's at stake. And

God is able to defend His name, His reputation. As I survey Scripture, it seems to me that those God uses the most are those who risk their reputation the most. They aren't afraid to ask God to make the sun stand still, walls fall down, or an iron ax head float.

The way you establish God's reputation is by risking your own. If you don't take the risk, you'll never witness the kind of miracles Bob did. God didn't just break the curse and resurrect the tree. It became the only tree of its type to yield its fruit not once but twice a year.

A double crop.

A double blessing.

A double miracle.

The Ultimate Apologetic

The seventh miracle reveals the true identity, the full identity of Jesus. He's not just Lord Latitude or Lord Algebra, as impressive as those miracles are. He's more than the Wine Maker or the Water Walker. He's the Grave Robber. And He saves His boldest claim for last:

I am the resurrection and the life.[6]

It's that unique claim that sets Jesus apart and puts Him in a category by Himself: the Son of God. Christianity is not built on the foundation of philosophy or a code of ethics. The footer of our faith is one fundamental fact—the empty tomb. After cheating death by calling Lazarus out of his tomb, Jesus walked out of His own tomb under His own power! That's the ultimate apologetic—there is no argument against it.

If the resurrection didn't happen, Christianity ranks as history's cruelest hoax. We're not just wasting our lives worshiping Him. We're living a lie. But if Jesus walked out of the tomb two thousand years ago, all bets are off. Or maybe I should say, all bets are on Jesus.

There is an old saying: *no one ever bet too much on a winning horse.* The winning horse is the White Horse that Jesus will ride when He returns for His church.[7]

Remember Jefferson's gospel? It comes to a dead end when the stone is rolled in front of the tomb on Good Friday. And I think that is where most people leave Jesus. Most people have no hesitation acknowledging that Jesus was compassionate and wise, a great teacher or a powerful prophet. But that isn't who He claimed to be. He claimed to be the resurrection and the life. And that's where many people get stuck. But we're only left with two options: either Jesus was who He claimed to be or He wasn't. There is no middle ground.

In an interview with *Rolling Stone* magazine, Bono was asked his opinion on Jesus with this question: "Christ has His rank among the world's greatest thinkers. But Son of God, isn't that far-fetched?" The lead singer of U2 and global crusader against poverty responded:

> No, it's not far-fetched to me. Look, the secular response to the Christ story always goes like this. He was a great prophet who had a lot to say along the lines of other great prophets, be they Elijah, Muhammad, Buddha, or Confucius. But actually Christ doesn't allow you that. He doesn't let you off that hook. Christ says, "No. I'm not saying I'm a teacher, don't call me a teacher. I'm not saying I'm a prophet. I'm saying: I'm the Messiah. I'm saying: I am God incarnate." And people say: No, no, please, just be a prophet. A prophet we can take. So what you're left with is either Christ was who He said he was—the Messiah—or a complete nutcase.[8]

Imagine a Jefferson vs. Bono debate. I'd pay-per-view to see that. I'm guessing the oddsmakers would make Jefferson the favorite by a long shot, but I think Bono wins this debate. While most people, like Jefferson, have no issue accepting Jesus as a compassionate healer or wise teacher or even a religious prophet, that isn't who He alleged to be. He claimed to be the Son of God. And as C. S. Lewis famously observed, Jesus is either a liar, a lunatic, or in fact who He claimed to be—Lord.[9]

There is no middle ground. Either Jesus is Lord of all or He's not Lord at all. So which is it? That one decision will determine your eternal destiny. It will also make the impossible possible!

25

ONE LITTLE YES

Do you believe this?

John 11:26

AFTER ASSERTING HIS identity as the resurrection and the life, Jesus pops a point-blank question that punctuates Martha's life: "Do you believe this?"[1] Remember: Jesus hadn't called Lazarus out of the tomb quite yet, so Martha was still in the depths of despair. Hope was four days dead. Yet Martha responds with her simple profession of faith:

Yes, Lord.[2]

One little *yes* can change your life.
One little *yes* can change your eternity.

The litmus test is the same now as it was then. The only question on God's final exam is: *Do you believe this?* It's not a multiple-choice question. It's true or false. And it's

262

the most important question you'll ever answer. That one decision will determine your eternal destiny. The good news is that it's an open-book exam, and God reveals the right answer in Romans 10:9:

> If you confess with your mouth that Jesus is Lord and believe in your heart that God raised him from the dead, you will be saved. (ESV)

The resurrection of Jesus Christ is the axis around which our faith revolves. When Jesus rose from the dead, it radically redefined reality. When He walked out of the tomb under His own power, the word *impossible* was removed from our vocabulary. The resurrection is the history-changer, the game-changer. But the trick is learning to live as if Jesus was crucified yesterday, rose from the dead today, and is coming back tomorrow![3]

The resurrection isn't something we celebrate once a year by donning an Easter bonnet. It's something we celebrate every day in every way. The resurrection of dead bodies is nothing short of miraculous, and the rematerialization of dead bodies when Christ returns is going to be must-see TV. But the resurrection miracles don't stop there. God raises dreams from the dead. He resurrects dead relationships. And no matter what part of your personality has died at the hands of sin or suffering or Satan himself, the Grave Robber came to give you your life back!

No one had laughed or smiled since the day Lazarus was laid to rest. When he walked out of the tomb, no one could stop. The seventh miracle is a snapshot of who Jesus is, what Jesus does. The Grave Robber steals back what the enemy has stolen. Then He gives it back to us, with interest.

A few years ago I had the privilege of baptizing a young woman whose life had been totally transformed by the grace of God. I'll never forget Rachel's face when she came back up out of the water. Pure joy! Rachel described it this way: "Now I'm the person I was as a child, always smiling and laughing."

When Jesus died on the cross, Satan smiled. But the Grave Robber got the last laugh. He always does. And if you give Him a chance, He'll give you a second chance.

He will give you your smile back.

He will give you your laugh back.

He will give you your life back.

Do you believe this?

If you do, He will make the impossible possible.

ACKNOWLEDGMENTS

IT'S IMPOSSIBLE TO express the full measure of gratitude to everyone who deserves it for the part they played in the creation of this book.

First and foremost, I thank my family. God has not just called me to write and to pastor. He's called our family. So thanks to my wife, Lora, and our three children, Parker, Summer, and Josiah.

A special thanks to my brother-in-law, Joel Schmidgall, who is part of our teaching team at National Community Church. His messages on miracles have inspired me and are undoubtedly interwoven into the pages of this book.

Huge thanks to the dream team at Baker Books who believed in this book as much as I did—Dwight Baker, Chad Allen, Twila Bennett, Jack Kuhatschek, David Lewis, Wendy Wetzel, Ruth Anderson, Michele Misiak, and Cheryl Van Andel.

Thanks to my agent, Esther Fedorkevich, and the team at the Fedd Agency.

Acknowledgments

Thanks to my assistant, Jennifer, for her help with the finishing touches.

Finally, it's a unique challenge writing a book about the One who has both saved me and called me. I'm eternally grateful for the day the Grave Robber said, "Mark, come out!"

NOTES

Chapter 1 The Day Water Blushed

1. I'm indebted to Dorothy L. Sayers for this sentiment from her 1942 essay "Why Work?"

Chapter 2 Miraculous

1. Gene Weingarten, "Pearls Before Breakfast," *Washington Post*, April 8, 2007, http://www.washingtonpost.com/wp-dyn/content/article/2007/04/04/AR2007040401721.html.

2. You can see this "Selective Attention Test" video posted by Daniel Simons at http://www.youtube.com/watch?v=vJG698U2Mvo. See Christopher Chabris and Daniel Simons, *The Invisible Gorilla: How Our Intuitions Deceive Us* (New York: Crown Publishers, 2010).

3. G. K. Chesterton, *Orthodoxy* (Nashville: Sam Torode Book Arts, 2008), 56.

4. Andrew Fraknoi, "How Fast Are You Moving When You Are Sitting Still?" *The Universe in the Classroom* 71 (Spring 2007), http://www.astrosociety.org/edu/publications/tnl/71/uitc071.pdf, http://www.astrosociety.org/edu/publications/tnl/71/howfast.html.

5. Carl Zimmer, "You're a Dim Bulb (And I Mean That in the Best Possible Way)," *The Loom* (blog), March 23, 2006, http://blogs.discovermagazine.com/loom/2006/03/23/youre-a-dim-bulb-and-i-mean-that-in-the-best-possible-way/#.UjNs67warzc.

6. Shlomo Katz, ed., Torah.org, *Hamaayan*, vol. X, no. 1, October 21, 1995, http://www.torah.org/learning/hamaayan/5756/bereishis.html.

Chapter 3 The Lost Miracles

1. For these and other facts about the Library of Congress, see "About the Library," Library of Congress, http://www.loc.gov/about/index.html.

2. Thomas Jefferson, The Thomas Jefferson Papers Series 1, General Correspondence, 1651–1827, Thomas Jefferson to John Adams, June 10, 1815, http://hdl.loc.gov/loc.mss/mtj.mtjbib022062.

3. Edwin Gaustad, *Sworn on the Altar of God* (Grand Rapids: Eerdmans, 1996), 129.

4. Ibid., 130.

5. See Joshua 3.

6. See 2 Kings 5:14.

7. Laurence Gonzales, *Deep Survival* (New York: W. W. Norton, 2003), 52–53.

8. Mark 9:24 ESV.

9. John 20:31.

10. The exact quote is, "Every now and then a man's mind is stretched by a new idea or sensation, and never shrinks back to its former dimensions." From Oliver Wendell Holmes, *The Autocrat of the Breakfast-Table* (Boston: James R. Osgood and Co., 1873); online at Project Gutenberg, http://www.gutenberg.org/ebooks/751.

Chapter 4 The Wine Maker

1. Luke 2:47 ESV.

2. Luke 23:34 ESV.

3. Graham Greene, *The Power and the Glory* (London: Vintage Books, 2005), chap. 1.

4. See Luke 2:19.

5. See Psalm 8:5.

6. See 1 Corinthians 14:3.

7. John 2:3 ESV.

Chapter 5 Six Stone Jars

1. Water ranges between 55–78 percent of body weight, with 65 percent being a median.

2. "Water Facts," Water.org, 2014, http://water.org/water-crisis/water-facts/water/, accessed January 6, 2014.

3. John 2:3 ESV.

4. Justin Voda, "Da Vinci-Inspired Pump Brings Water to Thousands," *OCCC Pioneer*, April 16, 2012, http://pioneer2010.occc.edu/index.php/clubs/68-clubs/2016-da-vinci-inspired-pump-brings-water-to-thousands.

5. Learn about the Water4 Foundation at http://water4.org/.

6. 1 John 2:27.

7. John 2:10 ESV.

8. "LEGO," Brickipedia.com, http://lego.wikia.com/wiki/LEGO, accessed January 7, 2014.

9. S.v. "ethanol fermentation," Wikipedia.com, modified December 31, 2013, http://en.wikipedia.org/wiki/Ethanol_fermentation.

10. Genesis 1:3.

11. Abraham Kuyper, "Sphere Sovereignty," in *Abraham Kuyper: A Centennial Reader*, James D. Bratt, ed. (Grand Rapids: Eerdmans, 1998), 488.

12. Colossians 1:16–17.

13. Matthew 26:28.

14. See Hebrews 9:22.
   15. 2 Corinthians 5:21.
   16. See Isaiah 51:17.

Chapter 6 One Nudge

1. Phil Robertson with Mark Schlabach, *Happy, Happy, Happy: My Life and Legacy as the Duck Commander* (Brentwood, TN: Howard, 2013), 109.
   2. See Matthew 20:30.
   3. See Mark 2:1–12.
   4. See John 6:1–14.
   5. Richard H. Thaler and Cass R. Sunstein, *Nudge: Improving Decisions about Health, Wealth, and Happiness* (New York: Penguin, 2009), 4.
   6. See Exodus 30:34.
   7. See Exodus 26:31.
   8. See Psalm 37:23.
   9. See Ephesians 2:10.
   10. See Romans 8:28.
   11. See Revelation 3:20.
   12. The Celtic Christians called the Holy Spirit *An Geadh-Glas* or "Wild Goose." I wrote about this extensively in *Wild Goose Chase: Reclaim the Adventure of Pursuing God* (Colorado Springs: Multnomah, 2008).
   13. Mark Batterson, *In a Pit with a Lion on a Snowy Day* (Sisters, OR: Multnomah, 2006), 12.

Chapter 7 Supernatural Synchronicity

1. Andrew Carroll, *Here Is Where: Discovering America's Great Forgotten History* (New York: Crown, 2013), 3.
   2. Genesis 50:20.
   3. Henry Greene, "Wherever You Go," Central Press newsletter, Central Presbyterian Church, October 2013, http://www.cpcmerced.org/uploads/CentralPressOctober2013.pdf.
   4. Matthew 10:29–31.
   5. Benjamin Franklin, "Speech to the Constitutional Convention," June 28, 1787. See "Religion and the Founding of the American Republic: Part VI: Religion and Federal Government," Library of Congress, http://www.loc.gov/exhibits/religion/rel06.html.
   6. See John 10:10.
   7. See 1 John 4:4.
   8. Romans 8:31.
   9. As quoted in Joe Carter, "Being on God's Side," *First Things*, December 22, 2010, http://www.firstthings.com/web-exclusives/2010/12/being-on-gods-side-an-open-letter-to-the-religious-right.
   10. Nick Vujicic, *Unstoppable: The Incredible Power of Faith in Action* (Colorado Springs: Waterbrook, 2012), 20.
   11. See Romans 8:28.

Chapter 8 God Speed

1. 2 Peter 3:8.

Chapter 9 The Seventh Hour

1. Tony Snesko, personal email to the author, used by permission.
2. Ibid.
3. Dallas Willard, *The Great Omission: Reclaiming Jesus's Essential Teachings on Discipleship* (Oxford, UK: Lion Hudson, 2006), 61.
4. See Luke 8:43–48.
5. See Luke 7:36–50.
6. See Mark 2:1–12.
7. See Mark 8:22–26.
8. Mark 8:25 ESV.
9. John 4:46.

Chapter 10 Very Superstitious

1. "The Unsolvable Math Problem," Snopes.com, updated June 28, 2011, http://www.snopes.com/college/homework/unsolvable.asp.
2. George Dantzig, http://en.wikipedia.org/wiki/George_Dantzig.
3. Matthew 19:26.
4. John 5:8.
5. Sarah Young, *Jesus Calling* (Nashville: Thomas Nelson, 2004), 243.
6. Email to the author, used by permission.
7. One of many versions of this story appears at "Ty Cobb," Baseball-statistics.com, http://www.baseball-statistics.com/HOF/Cobb.html.
8. See Joshua 10.
9. See 2 Kings 6.
10. See Luke 1.
11. See Matthew 14.
12. John 11:25.

Chapter 11 Self-Fulfilling Prophecies

1. Alan Deutschman, *Change or Die* (New York: Regan, 2007), 3.
2. Ibid., 4.
3. John 5:6.
4. See Luke 23:39.
5. See 2 Kings 5.
6. See Luke 8:42–48.
7. See John 21.
8. "Understanding Motion by Standing Still," Boston University, January 16, 1998, http://www.newswise.com/articles/understanding-motion-by-standing-still.
9. See Daniel 1. I also recommend *The Daniel Plan: 40 Days to a Healthier Life* by Rick Warren, Dr. Daniel Amen, and Dr. Mark Hyman (Grand Rapids: Zondervan, 2013).
10. See Romans 8:37.

11. See Zechariah 2:8.

12. See Isaiah 62:12.

13. See Romans 8:17.

14. See John 1:12.

15. See Matthew 16:18.

16. "They'll Put a Man on the Moon before I Hit a Home Run," Did You Know?, May 4, 2011, http://didyouknow.org/theyll-put-a-man-on-the-moon-before-i-hit-a-home-run/.

17. Alex Santoso, "Jim Carrey Once Wrote Himself a $10 Million Check," Neatorama, October 7, 2012, http://www.neatorama.com/2012/10/07/Jim-Carrey-Once-Wrote -Himself-a-10-Million-Check/.

18. Acts 3:6.

19. Thanks to Eugene Peterson for this idea, inspired by his book *A Long Obedience in the Same Direction: Discipleship in an Instant Society* (Downers Grove, IL: InterVarsity, 1980).

Chapter 12 The Rule Breaker

1. See Mendy Hecht, "How Far Am I Allowed to Walk on Shabbat?" Chabad.org, http://www.chabad.org/library/article_cdo/aid/484235/jewish/How-far-am-I-allowed -to-walk-on-Shabbat.htm.

2. Alvaro Pascual-Leone, Amir Amedi, Felipe Fregni, and Lotfi B. Merabet, "The Plastic Human Brain Cortex," *Annual Review of Neuroscience* 28 (2005):377–401, http:// brain.huji.ac.il/publications/Pascual-Leone_Amedi_et%20al%20Ann%20Rev%20 Neurosci%2005.pdf.

3. Attributed to Albert Einstein, as quoted in Alice Calaprice, ed., *The New Quotable Einstein* (Princeton: Princeton University Press, 2005), 292.

4. Quoted in Guy Kawasaki, *Rules for Revolutionaries* (New York: HarperCollins, 1999), 8.

5. Rolf Smith, *The Seven Levels of Change: The Guide to Innovation in the World's Largest Corporations* (Arlington, TX: Summit, 1997), 49.

6. Russell Stannard, *The God Experiment: Can Science Prove the Existence of God?* (London: Faber and Faber, 1999), 77.

7. See Philippians 4:13.

8. Hugh Ross, *Beyond the Cosmos: What Recent Discoveries in Astrophysics Reveal about the Glory and Love of God* (Orlando, FL: Signalman, 2010), 110.

9. See Ephesians 3:20.

Chapter 13 Two Fish

1. John 6:5.

2. John 6:5.

3. John 6:7.

4. Deborah A. Small, George Loewenstein, and Paul Slovic, "Sympathy and Callousness: The Impact of Deliberative Thought on Donations to Identifiable and Statistical Victims," *Organizational Behavior and Human Decision Processes* 102:2 (March 2007), 143–53.

5. John 6:9.

6. See Numbers 11.
7. Numbers 11:21–22.
8. See Psalm 50:10.
9. Luke 6:38.
10. Numbers 11:31–32.

Chapter 14 Lord Algebra

1. Oswald Chambers, *My Utmost for His Highest* (Grand Rapids: Discovery House, 2006), 13.
2. Matthew 6:11 NKJV.
3. See Exodus 16, particularly verses 18–19.
4. See 2 Kings 4.
5. See Exodus 13.
6. See Mark 4.
7. John 6:10.
8. John 6:6.
9. See Mark 8:1–10.
10. See Matthew 13:1–23.
11. Matthew 13:8.

Chapter 15 Count the Fish

1. For more information, visit www.kicheko.org.
2. See Luke 21:1–4.
3. See John 21:1–14.
4. Luke 5:5.

Chapter 16 The Water Walker

1. Mark 4:39 NKJV.
2. Lindsey Konkel, "Could Humans Walk on Water?" Livescience.com, June 29, 2010, http://www.livescience.com/32670-could-humans-walk-on-water.html.
3. Doron Nof, Ian McKeague, and Nathan Paldor, "Is There a Paleolimnological Explanation for 'Walking on Water' in the Sea of Galilee?" *Journal of Paleolimnology* 35 (2006), 417–39. The authors make an admission along with this assertion: "Whether this happened or not is an issue for religion scholars, archeologists, anthropologists, and believers to decide on. As natural scientists, we merely point out that unique freezing processes probably happened in that region several times during the last 12,000 years."
4. Al Seckel, "Al Seckel: Visual Illusions That Show How We (Mis)Think," TED. com, February 2004 (posted April 2007), http://www.ted.com/talks/al_seckel_says_our_brains_are_mis_wired.html.
5. Richard Restak, *Mozart's Brain and the Fighter Pilot: Unleashing Your Brain's Potential* (New York: Harmony, 2001), 92.
6. Mark Nepo, *The Book of Awakening* (San Francisco: Conari Press, 2000), 131.
7. "*Star Trek* Quotes," IMDB.com, 2014, http://www.imdb.com/title/tt0060028/quotes.
8. John 3:8 ESV.

Chapter 17 Dare the Devil

1. See Matthew 21:12–13.
2. Dorothy Sayers, *The Greatest Drama Ever Staged: Letters to a Diminished Church* (Nashville: Thomas Nelson, 2004).
3. See Mark 5:1–20.
4. 1 John 4:18 ESV.
5. John 6:18.
6. André Gide, *The Counterfeiters: A Novel*, trans. Dorothy Bussy (New York: Vintage Books, 1973), 353.
7. See John 6:19.

Chapter 18 Cut the Cable

1. "Otis Elevator Company," Wikipedia, accessed February 13, 2014, http://en.wiki pedia.org/wiki/Otis_Elevator_Company.
2. See Matthew 14:22–33.
3. See Mark 6:48.
4. John 1:48.
5. John 1:46, 49.
6. "George Washington: First Inaugural Address," *Inaugural Addresses of the Presidents of the United States* (Washington, DC: U.S. G.P.O, 1989); online at Bartleby.com, http://www.bartleby.com/124/pres13.html.
7. Wayne Whipple, *The Story of Young George Washington* (Philadelphia: Henry Altemus Company, 1918), 180.
8. David Barton, *The Bulletproof George Washington* (Aledo, TX: Wallbuilder Press, 1990), 50–51.
9. The treatment of Native Americans is a dark chapter in our history as a nation. The same can be said of the enslavement of Africans who arrived on our shores in chains. The lyrics from "America the Beautiful" are true: "God shed His grace on thee." Like every other nation, America is far from perfect. But a close look at our history reveals a providential subplot that is unforgettable.
10. Matthew 14:24 ESV.
11. Matthew 14:26 ESV.
12. Matthew 14:28 ESV.

Chapter 19 Never Say Never

1. Oliver Sacks, *The Island of the Colorblind* (New York: Vintage Books, 1998), 208.
2. Luke 11:34 ESV.
3. *Pneumatology* is theology of the Holy Spirit. *Soteriology* is theology of salvation. *Eschatology* is theology of the end times.
4. Albert Einstein, "Religion and Science," *New York Times Magazine*, November 9, 1930, 1–4; online at http://www.sacred-texts.com/aor/einstein/einsci.htm.
5. Quoted in David N. Menton, "The Eye," BestBibleScience.org, http://www.best biblescience.org/eye.htm.
6. Proverbs 20:12.

7. Bradley Voktek, "Are There Really as Many Neurons in the Human Brain as Stars in the Milky Way?," *Brain Metrics* (blog), May 20, 2013, http://www.nature.com /scitable/blog/brain-metrics/are_there_really_as_many.

Chapter 20 The Miracle League

1. See Matthew 9:20–22.
2. John Tiller, testimony at National Community Church, used by permission.
3. Ibid.
4. John 9:2.
5. John 9:3.
6. Hebrews 11:32–35.
7. Hebrews 11:35–38.
8. Max Lucado shares JJ's story in his book *You'll Get through This: Hope and Help for Your Turbulent Times* (Nashville: Thomas Nelson, 2013), 23–24.
9. Ibid., 28.
10. "Mississippi Television Station WCBI Airs Flame On Story," Flame On Blog, March 9, 2011, http://www.flameon.net/blog/mississippi-television-station-wcbi-airs -flame-on-story.aspx.
11. Quoted in ibid.
12. Dr. Martin Seligman, *Learned Optimism* (New York: A. A. Knopf, 1991).
13. See Romans 8:37.
14. Genesis 50:20.
15. Aldous Huxley, *Texts and Pretexts* (New York: W. W. Norton, 1962), 5.
16. Romans 8:28.

Chapter 21 Spit on It

1. Greg Stielstra, *PyroMarketing: The Four-Step Strategy to Ignite Customer Evangelists and Keep Them for Life* (New York: HarperBusiness, 2005), 92.
2. John 9:39 NKJV.
3. John 8:12.
4. Genesis 1:3.
5. Genesis 1:2 ESV.
6. See John 9:6.
7. See Genesis 2:7.
8. See John 9:7.
9. As quoted by Rodney Buchanan in his sermon "Blindness and Light," Sermon Central, July 2007, http://www.sermoncentral.com/sermons/blindness--light-rodney -buchanan-sermon-on-faith-general-109700.asp.
10. John 9:7 ESV.

Chapter 22 The Grave Robber

1. Genesis 2:17.
2. John 11:44.
3. See 2 Corinthians 1:20.

4. "What Happened to Lazarus after His Resurrection?" The Straight Dope, October 20, 2009, http://www.straightdope.com/columns/read/2902/what-happened-to-lazarus-after-his-resurrection.

5. See John 10:10.

6. 1 Corinthians 15:55.

7. See 2 Corinthians 5:8.

Chapter 23 Even Now

1. John 11:15.

2. John 11:21, 32.

3. John 11:4.

4. Oswald Chambers, "The Big Compelling of God," in *My Utmost for His Highest*, http://utmost.org/classic/the-big-compelling-of-god-classic/.

5. John 11:21–22.

6. Ibid.

7. See John 11:21.

8. See Psalm 56:8.

9. See Proverbs 18:24.

Chapter 24 Risk Your Reputation

1. Clayton told me this story in person, but you can read his amazing account in his book *Amazing Encounters with God: Stories to Open Your Eyes to His Power* (Eugene, OR: Harvest House, 2009).

2. John 11:43.

3. See Daniel 3.

4. Daniel 3:16–18.

5. Daniel 3:27 NLT.

6. John 11:25.

7. See Revelation 19:11.

8. Michka Assayas, *Bono: In Conversation with Michka Assayas* (New York: Riverhead, 2005), 205.

9. C. S. Lewis, *Mere Christianity* (1952; New York: HarperCollins, 2001), 54.

Chapter 25 One Little Yes

1. See John 11:25–26.

2. John 11:27 NLT.

3. Thanks to Martin Luther for this thought. He said, "Preach as if Jesus was crucified yesterday, rose from the dead today, and is coming back tomorrow."

Mark Batterson is the *New York Times* bestselling author of *The Circle Maker*. The lead pastor of National Community Church in Washington, DC, Mark has a doctor of ministry degree from Regent University and lives on Capitol Hill with his wife, Lora, and their three children.

Find your resources for individuals and small groups at

MARKBATTERSON.COM

You will find...

Sermon outlines

Church resources

Printable bookmarks, postcards, etc.

...

Connect with

MARK
BATTERSON

at

MarkBatterson.com

🐦 @MarkBatterson

f Mark Batterson

📷 @MarkBatterson

Connect with National Community Church at
WWW.THEATERCHURCH.COM

"Mark reminds us that faith in Jesus is worth the risk."

–Max Lucado, pastor and bestselling author

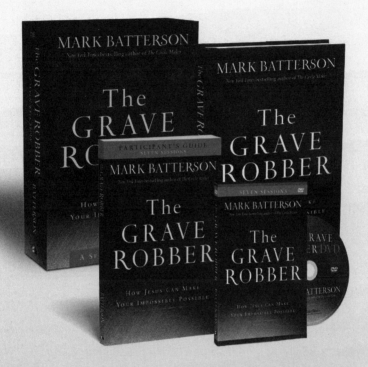

Perfect for a church-wide experience or a small group. *The Grave Robber* will help congregations discover that **God can still do the impossible**.